Protecting Aboriginal Children

Christopher Walmsley

Protecting Aboriginal Children

UBCPress · Vancouver · Toronto

15 14   5 4 3

Printed in Canada on ancient-forest-free paper (100% post-consumer recycled) that is processed chlorine- and acid-free, with vegetable-based inks.

Library and Archives Canada Cataloguing in Publication

Walmsley, Christopher
  Protecting Aboriginal children / Christopher Walmsley.

Includes bibliographical references and index.
ISBN 13: 978-0-7748-1170-5 (bound); 978-0-7748-1171-2 (pbk.)
ISBN 10: 0-7748-1170-6 (bound); 0-7748-1171-4 (pbk.)

   1. Indian children – Services for – British Columbia. 2. Child welfare – British Columbia. 3. Child welfare workers – British Columbia. I. Title.

HV745.B7W34 2005   362.7'089'970711   C2005-905415-8

Canadä

UBC Press gratefully acknowledges the financial support for our publishing program of the Government of Canada through the Book Publishing Industry Development Program (BPIDP), and of the Canada Council for the Arts, and the British Columbia Arts Council.

UBC Press
The University of British Columbia
2029 West Mall
Vancouver, BC V6T 1Z2
604-822-5959 / Fax: 604-822-6083
www.ubcpress.ca

To Lise, who will always be my favourite child protection
social worker, for her support from the very beginning to the end.

To my parents, Helen Emma Dixon and Hilary John Walmsley,
whose love of people, respect for difference, independence, originality,
and perseverance gave me the qualities that made this book possible.

Contents

Foreword
Bill Simon

I was very pleased to be given the opportunity of writing a foreword to this important book – a book that will prove to be of great value to students, researchers, and practitioners in the field of social development. The ideas and insights focus on what social work practice is like when working with the Aboriginal community, but the lessons learned can be used in the ongoing development of innovative social work models in all fields of socioeconomic development.

This book comes when the development and delivery of Aboriginal-controlled social work programs and services is emerging and growing in North America and in other areas such as New Zealand and Australia. Aboriginals in these parts of the world have always been overrepresented within the negative context of social development. There is a disproportionate number of Aboriginal children in the child welfare system and the conditions of Aboriginal peoples in these First World countries are no better than are conditions for people in Third World countries.

Aboriginal social work practice is not just about developing social work processes geared towards an understanding of Aboriginal perspectives; rather, it is about using this perspective to develop and implement social work theory as the kind of standards that accompany any social development programming. Social work practitioners really need to stop telling people what they think is right for them and start listening to what the people themselves think will work for them. Respect for other people's cultures and practices is usually the first step in understanding where they are coming from and how they would like to resolve their ongoing issues. The key is to ensure that outsiders do not interject their own perceptions into what the clients are actually saying. If social workers approach Aboriginal people in a respectful and meaningful manner, then they will be able to begin the process of putting in place a practice that is driven by the grassroots of the communities they serve. This kind of practice ensures that social programming is developed from within rather than from without. It is the kind of practice that looks towards making legislation, policies, and rules and regulations work for the people rather than towards making the latter work for the former. If this were to happen, then perhaps we could stop telling people what we think is right for them.

When the agency I currently work for held its official opening ceremonies on 17 October 2000, the affiliated seven First Nations communities signed "A Proclamation to Secwepemc Children," which, in part, stated: "On behalf of the Secwepemc People, we stand before this assembly of Secwepemc Children and make a solemn proclamation that child abuse and child neglect are not acceptable in our communities. We pledge to uphold the sacredness of Secwepemc Children, and that we will seek and ensure to the best of our abilities, the justice and respect that is rightfully yours, to be passed down to future generations for all times."

We operate and strive to honour that historical document because that is the basis of the mandate given to us by the First Nations with whom we work. In the Aboriginal community the process used in the delivery of child welfare services is owned by the members of the community, and I like to say that our bosses are the children of those communities. It is the children to whom I listen when I look at making plans for their benefit; after all, what we decide on their behalf is what they have to live with. And, in respecting their wishes, we show that we value their input and honour their sacredness.

The words "honour," "justice," "respect," and "sacredness" should become the standard vocabulary of people who want to become proficient in their practice of social work. Using those words as a guide will enable you to keep focused on what needs to be done and will enable you to remind yourself of the sacredness of children, which will truly guide you towards the right path. Honouring children and being respectful in your approach towards this sometimes gut-wrenching field of work will enable you to get closer to achieving the trust that is so lacking, but so necessary, when working with children and families. Without this trust you would merely be administering policies and procedures – something that could be done by pencil pushers rather than social workers.

For far too long Aboriginal children have not received the justice and respect that is owed to them, and *Protecting Aboriginal Children* will go a long way toward rectifying this situation. Dr. Christopher Walmsley has approached the subject of social work practice in the Aboriginal community by paying the utmost respect to the historical perspectives of Aboriginal peoples. He is aware of past social injustices and looks at how justice and respect can be intertwined with the practice of social work. This book is one more step towards gaining a better understanding of a vast array of issues that are being dealt with in the Aboriginal community. Good research is in demand as it will result in a better education for future social workers who want to work with Aboriginal people. When it comes to social programming, collaborative research between academia and the Aboriginal community is necessary to ensure that the former becomes more sensitive and responsive to the needs of Aboriginal communities.

Caring for children is every community's most important job. The first and greatest investment in time and resources should be devoted to the care and treatment of children in their own home and, when that is not possible, in their own communities.

Read this book with an open mind and do not forget about honour, justice, respect, and the sacredness of children.

Bill Simon is a member of the Elsipogtog First Nation (Mi'kmaq), New Brunswick. He was the first executive director of the Secwepemc Child and Family Services Agency (2000-5), serving seven Secwepemc First Nation Communities in Kamloops, BC. In addition, he was the first executive director of the Scw'exmx Child and Family Services Agency (1994-98), serving five Nicola Valley First Nations near Merritt, BC. Currently, he is working for the All Nations Trust Company/All Nations Development Corporation as a business development officer.

Acknowledgments

I wish to thank the following people for their support. Dr. Jacques Vachon taught me clarity and simplicity in research design at the beginning of this project. Jean Wilson, from UBC Press, provided early interest, ongoing encouragement, and practical advice as the book developed. Mary Ann Peressini spent many hours transforming audiotaped interviews to text.

I also wish to acknowledge the financial support received during this research.

I received a National Welfare Fellowship from Health and Welfare Canada (now Human Resources Canada), support funds from the School of Social Work, Laval University, and special project funds from the University College of the Cariboo (now Thompson Rivers University). The support of these sponsors has been invaluable to the completion of this work.

Protecting Aboriginal Children

1
Introduction

In the fall of 1996 I began teaching social work at the University College of the Cariboo (now Thompson Rivers University) in Kamloops, British Columbia. On a warm September day, a community forum met to discuss potential changes to child welfare policy in our region. The changes, proposed by Judge Thomas Gove, emerged from his judicial inquiry into the death of five-year-old Matthew Vaudreuil. His extensive three-volume report recommended many changes but devoted almost no attention to First Nations children, although they comprise 40 percent of the children in the care of the Province of British Columbia. At that forum an Aboriginal woman came to the microphone and passionately asked why that was the case. Responses were not forthcoming. Her speech and the relative silence that followed were vivid testimony to the fact that, once more, Aboriginal people were left out of the account – in this case, an influential judicial inquiry into the operation of British Columbia's child welfare system.

This book addresses the silence found in the Gove Inquiry Report and the academic and professional child welfare literature concerning Aboriginal children's welfare. While Aboriginal children constitute 40 percent or more of the children in state care in western and northern Canada, attention devoted to child protection practice is sparse. Statistics on the rates of Aboriginal children in care are available, but knowledge about the practice of child protection investigation and decision making with regard to Aboriginal children is generally unavailable.

Protecting Aboriginal Children aims to explain child protection practice from the vantage point of the social worker – the person who does the work of child protection. It is the result of nineteen in-depth interviews conducted in 1998 and 1999 with BC child protection workers, all of whom had extensive contact with Aboriginal children and families. Aboriginal and non-Aboriginal social workers – those who work for

Aboriginal child welfare organizations and those who work for the BC Ministry of Children and Family Development – were interviewed. All participants had a social work education, two or more years of full-time child protection practice experience, and ongoing responsibility for making protection decisions with regard to Aboriginal children. All lived and worked in reserve communities, small towns, or regional BC town centres. By examining how they talk and think about their practice, I explore how social workers actually practice child protection.

Since the late 1950s Aboriginal children have been significantly overrepresented in Canadian child welfare systems. Between 1955 and 1964, for example, the percentage of Aboriginal children in the care of the Province of British Columbia jumped from less than 1 percent to 34.2 percent, and this pattern was repeated in other parts of Canada during the same time (Johnston 1983). In 1996 the Royal Commission on Aboriginal Peoples (RCAP) found that "the percent of First Nations children in care is six times that of children from the general population in the care of public agencies" (RCAP 1996, 3:32). It noted that this disparity has increased since the 1970s.

Two fundamental responses have occurred since the 1980s in response to this sociopolitical reality. Political action by First Nations governments created various models of child welfare service managed by the Aboriginal community. These include tripartite agreements (between the Canadian government, a province, and First Nations communities), agreements between a province and a band, and regional Aboriginal services delivered by boards under Aboriginal control (RCAP 1996, 3:30). In addition, existing child welfare policy and procedure have been modified in a number of provinces to recognize in some way the significance of cultural identity when intervening with First Nations children. This ranges from informing a child of their Aboriginal status and consulting with the child's community before wardship hearings (Alberta), to considering the child's cultural and religious heritage in determining her/his best interests (Newfoundland), to taking into consideration the characteristics of Native communities (Quebec), and to considering a child's cultural background and "lifestyle in home community" in adoption cases (Yukon). Under the term "Native," Ontario, the province with the most extensive provisions for Aboriginal child welfare, includes status Indian people and others of Aboriginal ancestry in its legislation. It also recognizes "Indian" and "Native status" as a "best interests" category over and above the obligation to consider cultural background (RCAP 1996, 3:31).

In spite of these modest changes, whose purpose is to recognize the needs of Aboriginal families and communities, the nature of child welfare practice as it relates to Aboriginal children in Canada is essentially unknown. Descriptions and evaluations of organizational models, programs, and services are available (Wharf 2002; McKenzie 1989, 1997; McKenzie, Seidl, and Bone 1995; Armitage 1993a; Armitage, Lane, Ricks, and Wharf 1988; Hudson and Taylor-Henley 1987; Hudson and McKenzie 1987; Hume 1991; Hart 1992; Damm 1992; Wares, Wedel, Rosenthal, and Dobrec 1994; Hodgson 1993), but knowledge about practice in child protection, particularly within a cross-cultural context, is unavailable.

Research on child protection practice more generally has focused on the decision to remove a child from the family and place him or her in substitute care. This decision is universally regarded as an "awesome responsibility" for the social worker – one with far-reaching consequences for the child. However, as Briar noted in 1963, "systematically we know next to nothing about how the child-placement worker makes these decisions" (Lindsey 1992, 76). A review of the literature three decades later concluded that "knowledge in the child welfare field does not provide a scientific knowledge base for discerning where to draw the line on cases best served in home and those needing out-of-home care" (ibid.). Decision making appears to be influenced by "ideologies of workers, agencies, and courts" (Jones 1993, 253), the mother's preference, resource availability, idiosyncratic decisions of the worker, funding patterns, and organizational characteristics of social service bureaucracies rather than the needs of the child or parent (Lindsey 1992). The absence of "a constant set of principles that guide practitioners in making decisions" led one researcher to conclude: "It is not surprising, therefore, that reliability in decision making is poor and that individual discretion and personal bias have been found to exert a strong influence on the decision-making behaviour of child welfare staff" (Stein and Rzepnicki in Lindsey 1992, 77).

Lack of an adequate scientific knowledge base with which to decide whether to remove a child from her/his parents leads one author to argue that such decision making is fundamentally moral (Lindsey 1992, 77). Although some recognize that there is a moral, or normative, dimension to decision making in child protection, social work ethics places little emphasis on questions related to this area. A survey of social work ethics texts (Loewenberg and Dolgoff 1992; Reamer 1995; Rhodes 1991) reveals no case examples specific to child protection. While the profession recognizes the social control dimension to practice in the professional literature (Hutchison 1987; Palmer 1983; Groulx 1995), it does not address the ethical issues arising from such practice within the context of state relations to a subordinated cultural minority.

Child protection practice is structured, oriented, and justified within a regulatory framework comprising legislation, policy, and resources. This framework informs a range of normative conceptions that serve to privilege some practice approaches over others. These conceptions provide interpretations of need, describe policy goals, and circumscribe intervention. They also provide a level of conceptual orientation and guidance to practitioner action. In naming the ideas that orient action, language plays a key role. It defines social reality, interprets people's inchoate aspirations and needs, and gives voice to political struggles about needs, rights, and resources (Fraser and Gordon 1994, 310). Professional language also plays a role since "it is never an independent instrument or simply a tool for description" (Edelman 1984, 44). It helps to create social relationships and marshals "public support for professional and governmental practices that have profound political consequences" (ibid.). Particular words or expressions can often become the focal point of differences about intervention strategy or method. They function as "keywords, sites at which the meaning of social experience is negotiated and contested. Keywords typically carry unspoken assumptions and connotations that can powerfully influence the discourses they permeate – in part by constituting a body of doxa, or taken-for-granted commonsense belief that escapes critical scrutiny" (Fraser and Gordon 1994, 310).

While child welfare policy has the universally recognized goal of ensuring the safety and well-being of children, differences in orientation are visible in the language used to describe this goal. There are differences regarding legislation and policy, what resources to provide, and what intervention strategy to use. This debate takes place at either the case or policy level and implies a preference for some practice approaches over others.

In the child welfare literature the fundamental choice in policy orientation is sometimes described as a dichotomy between child rescue and family rehabilitation (Nelson 1984, 8, 9), child protection versus family support (Purvey 1991, 108; Savoury and Kufeldt, 1997; Mannes 1993), or the child's best interests versus family reunification (Weisman 1994, 47). These dichotomies suggest different approaches to the interpretation of children's needs, the focus of intervention, and the provision of resources. If the focus is exclusively the child, then this implies a policy orientation that conceptualizes children as autonomous beings increasingly capable of self-direction. This view can be extended to argue that children have rights and that the state has a duty to ensure these rights. If parents are unable to provide adequate medical services, housing, education, nutrition, and protection, then the duty to fulfill this right falls to the state.

A family-focused policy orientation suggests that a child's needs are best met within the context of a family, and social intervention should be directed to enable families to adequately care for children. Social intervention to support the family can include income, housing, health care, daycare, parent education, and counselling (Armitage 1993b, 55). More specifically, when a child is at risk of neglect or abuse, social intervention can involve a range of family centred, home-based protective services. Known as family preservation services, these include intensive casework with the mother, daycare for the children, and homemakers. They are aimed at placement prevention and family reunification (Frankel 1988, 139). These programs arose in response to social science findings concerning the adequacy of the state to protect and nurture children when parents are unable to do so. Central to social scientists' concerns were the limitations of the foster care system. The first large-scale study of foster care, completed in 1959 by Henry Maas and Richard Engler, "found that the children removed from their biological parents and placed with a foster family on what was to be a 'temporary' basis often lingered in foster care for an indeterminate number of years" (Lindsey 1994, 28). This finding was supported by David Fanshel and Eugen Shinn's 1965 study of New York foster care. They found that most children spent years in foster care before getting out. In the interim, the home situation had not improved and the families' economic situation had often deteriorated (Lindsey 1994, 33): "The most important determinant of how well children did in foster care was parental visiting. Those children who were visited by their parents while in foster care showed greater improvement and were most likely to be restored to their parent(s) than were children who were rarely visited by their parent(s)" (34). These studies and others initiated a reappraisal of the significance of the family in the care and development of children.

A third orientation to child welfare policy is becoming more evident in the literature, and it has particular significance for Aboriginal people (Wharf 2002; Burford and Hudson 2000). Encapsulated by the phrase "it takes a whole community to raise a child" this orientation highlights the significance of the community to the fulfillment of children's needs. Aboriginal peoples view the community as integral to identity formation: a cultural identity is accomplished only through active participation in and connection to the communal ties that constitute the culture. The opposite of this – subordination to or assimilation within the dominant culture – negatively affects identity. Assimilation and subordination harm a child's development and can lead to depression, suicide, and alcoholism (Sandberry 1992; Timpson 1988; Walmsley 1987).

Cultural autonomy with respect to the care of children is essential to the survival of Aboriginal peoples. There are three central elements to cultural autonomy. First, it is important to participate in extended family relationships. The kinship unit, not the biological parents, has the primary responsibility for childcare. "Uncles and aunts were like parents, and a niece or nephew could help her or himself to things without getting scolded" (Ramsay 1986, 14). Second, it is important to be aware of the teachings of elders. Elders have great significance because of their knowledge of traditional values and their wisdom about life. Part of the search for identity and cultural autonomy involves understanding these values and being able to apply them in a modern context. Third, it is important to recognize a spiritual dimension to life. Spirituality is viewed as essential to being in harmony with the world. An active spiritual life is also essential to avoid depression, anomie, and normlessness (Timpson 1988). These beliefs about living inform an approach to cultural survival, to family life and childcare, and to child welfare policy. They are often encapsulated in the positive evaluation of community and suggest a communitarian orientation to child welfare policy.

The majority of social workers engaged in child protection practice are women, but it is not clear how much influence gender might have on thinking about child protection practice with regard to Aboriginal children. Women describe child protection practice as complex, fast-paced, unsafe, invisible, and undervalued, and they maintain that crucial life decisions are made within a context of contradictory roles (Callahan 1993, 73). The regulatory framework within which practice takes place is a political/judicial/bureaucratic system governed by men (Pateman 1988). Corporate management approaches increasingly codify child protection work and centralize decision making (Callahan 1993). Child protection, practised predominantly by women with women and children, can be viewed as an extension of women's traditional caring role in society. Although the practice might involve women-to-women dialogues about childcare, mothering, safety, and protection, an understanding of the ideas that actually inform women's child protection practice is not evident in the literature.

Today, child protection takes place within different organizational contexts and is practised by women and men as well as by Aboriginal and non-Aboriginal social workers. However, the thinking that informs practice with Aboriginal children has not been explored.

Protecting Aboriginal Children begins with an overview of historical issues concerning child protection practice as it relates to Aboriginal children in Canada (Chapter 2). It then goes on to summarize the evolution of provincial child welfare policy and services in British Columbia (Chapter 3), the province in which the interviews took place. Next it provides an in-depth description of child protection practice, quoting extensively from interviews with child protection social workers (Chapter 4). In order to protect the anonymity of the interviewees, I provide no names, dates, or other identifying information. The succeeding chapters explore the sociopolitical context (Chapter 5), organizational context (Chapter 6), and community context (Chapter 7) of practice. Chapter 8 describes how social workers envision the ideals of practice, and it analyzes the explanations they provide for intervention. It concludes with a discussion of the knowledge base of practice. Chapter 9 describes practitioners' thinking about the choices involved in practice action. The book concludes by identifying four social representations of child protection practice – power, policy, family, and community representations – with recommendations for research, policy, and practice arising from an understanding of these.

While *Protecting Aboriginal Children* is a study of child protection practice, it also aims to engage readers without an extensive research background. To accomplish this, the theoretical perspective and methodology have been placed in appendices. Readers with a particular interest in these aspects of the book are advised to read the appendices before moving to the next chapter, which will provide an overview of the theoretical and methodological dimensions of the study as well as the rationale for the chapters.

2
The Historical Context

The coercive power of the state meets the family through
the social practice of child protection. The symbol of this relationship is the social worker, whose power permits the forcible
separation of a child from parents, siblings, or cultural community. The stated objective of such intervention is the protection
of the best interests of the child, and this often means trying
to determine the least harmful, disruptive, or detrimental
alternative for the child's care.

– David A. Cruickshank, *The Child in Care*

Aboriginal families and communities first encountered the coercive
power of the Canadian state when the Indian Act was passed in 1876.
The Indian Act preceded, by three-quarters of a century, the introduction of Aboriginal children into provincial child welfare systems. It con-
tained a series of assimilationist and integrationist policies designed to
turn Aboriginal peoples into ordinary Canadian citizens. The Indian
Act, created to consolidate previous legislation dealing with Indians
in the provinces and territories, fundamentally changed the legal position of Aboriginal peoples and dramatically influenced European-
Indian relations on into the twenty-first century. For Aboriginal peoples,
it prohibited:

- the acquisition of land or meaningful control of land use (1876 to the
  present)
- voting in federal elections (until 1960)
- voting in provincial elections (until 1949)
- voting in municipal elections (until 1948)

- participation in potlatches (1884-1951)
- participation in festivals and dances (1895-1951)
- possession of alcohol on reserve or intoxication on or off reserve (1876-1970)
- sale of agricultural products without permission (1881 to the present)
- prosecuting land claims or retaining a lawyer (1927-51).
  (Mathias and Yabsley 1991, 40-45)

Aboriginal women were doubly disadvantaged under the Indian Act, particularly with respect to land surrender, wills, band elections, Indian status, band membership, and enfranchisement (RCAP 1996, 1:300). The Indian Act consolidated the creation of reserve lands throughout Canada and also provided for a separate Indian education system.

The cornerstone of the government's cultural assimilation strategy was the education policy of residential schools. Incorporating childcare and education, this policy aimed to civilize, Christianize, and socialize Aboriginal children to work in the wage economy. The aim of the residential school policy was to erase Aboriginal identity by separating generations of children from their families, suppressing their Aboriginal languages, and resocializing them according to the norms of non-Aboriginal society (RCAP 1996, 1: chap. 10). In summary, the residential school policy was "designed to move communities, and eventually all Aboriginal peoples, from their helpless 'savage' state to one of self-reliant 'civilization' and thus to make in Canada but one community – a non-Aboriginal, Christian one" (RCAP 1996, 1:333). The deputy superintendent general of Indian Affairs, Duncan Campbell Scott, told the House of Commons in 1920: "Our object is to continue until there is not a single Indian in Canada that has not been absorbed into the body politic and there is no Indian question, and no Indian department, that is the whole object of this Bill" (Haig-Brown 1988, 27).

Informally, residential schools also served as the Canadian government's child welfare service for Aboriginal peoples until the 1950s. Beginning in 1879 two types of schools were constructed. There were boarding schools, built close to reserve communities, and centrally located industrial schools. RCAP (1996, 1:337) found that

the tragic legacy of residential education began in the late nineteenth century with a three-part vision of education in the service of assimilation. It included, first, a justification for removing children from their communities and disrupting Aboriginal families, second, a precise pedagogy for re-socializing children in the schools, and third, schemes for integrating graduates into the non-Aboriginal world.

With the enthusiastic participation of the Anglican, Roman Catholic, Methodist, and Presbyterian churches, the system grew at the rate of two schools per year; and by 1904 sixty-four schools had been constructed. A total of eighty schools were in operation by 1931 and could be found in all provinces except Prince Edward Island, New Brunswick, and Newfoundland. Sixteen schools were built in British Columbia.

Throughout its history, the residential school system was chronically underfunded and provided substandard education, housing, health care, and childcare. "As late as 1950, over 40 percent of the teaching staff had no professional training" (RCAP 1996, 1:345). Twenty-four percent of the student population died from tuberculosis in the early twentieth century, and "this figure might have risen to 42 per cent if the children had been tracked for three years after they returned to their reserves." Buildings were fire hazards and had inadequate wiring, heating, and plumbing. Children's diets lacked sufficient A, B, and C vitamins and had too little meat, green vegetables, grains, fruits, eggs, and milk (RCAP 1996, 1:357-62). As late as 1953 the focus of residential school discipline policy "remained on strapping, and other forms of punishment

Table 1

Indian residential schools in British Columbia

School	Years of operation
St. Mary's Mission	1863 to 1984
Coqualeetza	1888 to 1941
Kamloops	1890 to 1978
Kuper Island	1890 to 1975
Kootenay	1890 to 1970
Port Simpson	1890 to 1948
Cariboo	1891 to 1981
Alberni	1891 to 1973
Kitimaat	1893 to 1941
Christie	1900 to 1983
St. George's	1901 to 1978
Squamish	1902 to 1960
Ahousaht	1904 to 1939
Sechelt	1905 to 1975
Lejac	1910 to 1976
Alert Bay	1929 to 1974 or 1975

Sources: Fortin (1998); York (1990).

that continued to be commonly applied – confinement and depriva-
tion of food, head shaving, and public beatings – were not specifically
prohibited" (RCAP 1996, 1:372). In the 1990s the revelation of sexual
abuse of children by residential school employees opened a new chapter in the destructive legacy of the schools. Rix Rogers, special advisor to
the minister of national health and welfare on child sexual abuse, commented that "closer scrutiny of treatment of children at residential
schools would show that all children at some schools were sexually
abused" (RCAP 1996, 1:378).

RCAP (1996, 1:342) argued that, fundamentally, there were two residential school policies:

> The first in the long period before the Second World War placed the
> school at the heart of the strategy to disestablish communities through
> assimilation. In the subsequent period, the residential school system
> served a secondary role in support of the integration of children into the
> provincial education system and the modernization of communities.

The residential schools became "a supplementary service for children
who for very special reasons cannot commute to federal day schools or
provincial schools from their homes." It was during this period that the
child welfare function of the residential school became visible. In 1943
the "need for residential places for orphans and children from disrupted
homes" was not an unforeseen implication of the new integration policy.
A new admissions policy was developed, and it was "based on the circumstances of the student's family." In situations where federal day schools
or integration was possible, priority was to be given to children "from
families where a serious problem leading to neglect of children exists."
A 1966 Indian Affairs Department report estimated that 75 percent of the
children in residential schools "were from homes which, by reasons of
overcrowding and parental neglect or indifference, are considered unfit
for school children" (RCAP 1996, 1:348, 349).

In 1948 60 percent of the Indian school population attended federal
schools, but by 1969 60 percent were enrolled in provincial schools.
The number of residential schools dropped from seventy-two in 1948
to twelve in 1979. By 1986 the Department of Indian Affairs was virtually at "the end of the residential school road" (RCAP 1996, 1:351).

Until the 1980s residential schools operated outside the consciousness of the Euro-Canadian public. In British Columbia only one public
inquiry considered conditions in a residential school. This was a coro-
ner's inquest into the death of eight-year-old Duncan Sticks, who ran

away from the Williams Lake Residential School in 1902 and was found dead the next day (Furniss 1992). In British Columbia all schools were located in rural areas, whereas the province's Euro-Canadian population was concentrated in the urban regions of Vancouver and Victoria. The centres of government, media, higher education, and social reform were many kilometres away.

Today, residential schools evoke powerful memories for the schools' survivors, their families, and communities. Survivors remember being called derogatory names by staff, being sexually abused, being given bread and water as punishment for speaking their language, having letters censored, enduring chronic hunger, having their heads shaved, and being called heathens (Furniss 1992, 110; Haig-Brown 1988, 76; MacDonald 1993, 13; RCAP 1996, 2: Chap. 2, 35). One BC band chief summarizes the effects of the residential school in her community:

> Later when these children returned home, they were aliens. They did not speak their own language, so they could not communicate with anyone other than their own counterparts. Some looked down on their families because of their lack of English, their lifestyle, and some were just plain hostile. They had formed no bonds with their families, and some couldn't survive without the regimentation they had become so accustomed to ... Perhaps the greatest tragedy of this background was the unemotional upbringing they had. Not being brought up in a loving, caring, sharing, nurturing environment, they did not have these skills as they are not inbred but learned through observation, participation, and interaction. Consequently, when these children became parents, and most did at an early age, they had no parenting skills. They did not have the capability to show affection. They sired and bred children, but were unable to relate to them on any level. (Chief Cinderina Williams of the Spallumcheen Band, RCAP 1996, 3: Chap. 2, 35)

The residential school experience was the most powerful common issue raised by Aboriginal peoples across Canada in their presentations to the Royal Commission on Aboriginal Peoples (Furniss 1992, 31). There is now a growing body of literature concerning the schools that documents the policies, practices, and experiences of oppression (Fournier and Crey 1997; Miller 1996; Furniss 1992; Haig-Brown 1988; York 1990). Currently, 6,700 residential school survivors are involved in lawsuits, and an additional 550 survivors are involved in alternative dispute resolution processes directed at the Canadian government and Canadian churches, which provided residential education to Aboriginal children

(Assembly of First Nations, Ottawa, 2004). However, as the residential schools closed, the number of Aboriginal children admitted to provincial child welfare resources increased dramatically.

The division of powers in the Canadian Constitution can explain, in part, the transformation of Aboriginal child welfare services from church-state residential school to provincial child welfare authority. First Nations peoples in Canada, and specifically status Indians, are recognized as a federal responsibility, whereas children and families who receive social assistance are recognized as a provincial responsibility. The federal government has historically "declined to introduce services (other than education) on Indian reserves in parallel with provincial institutions" (RCAP 1996, 3:34, 37):

> The provinces have been reluctant to extend services to reserves principally because of the costs involved, but also because many First Nations have not welcomed provincial involvement, fearing that engaging in a relationship with the province might compromise their relationship with the federal government and their entitlements under treaties.

Although a 1951 amendment to the Indian Act provided that all laws of general application in force in a province apply on-reserve unless they conflict with a federal law or treaty, this did little to augment social service planning for Aboriginal peoples. "Except on an emergency basis, child welfare services were generally not available to Indian people living on reserve" (RCAP 1996, 3:38). When provided, these services were based on a non-Aboriginal value system and worldview.

The federal government was closing residential schools during the 1960s and, at the same time, signing the Canada Assistance Plan with the provinces. This fifty-fifty cost-sharing agreement provided provincial social services, and now "non-status Indians, Métis people, and off-reserve Status Indians were clearly within the ambit of provincial services" (RCAP 1996, 3:38). However, the ongoing jurisdictional dispute between the federal government and the provincial governments left status Indians on-reserve without service (Johnston 1983, 4). The principal response of provincial child welfare authorities during the 1960s was the apprehension and removal of Aboriginal children from their families and communities. Known as the "sixties scoop," social workers explained their actions by arguing that they were in the best interests of the children. "They felt that the apprehension of Indian children from reserves would save them from the effects of crushing poverty, unsanitary health conditions, poor housing and malnutrition, which were facts of life on many reserves" (23). Most children were placed in non-Aboriginal foster homes or care facilities, but a significant number were adopted. Between 1971 and 1981 75 percent were adopted into non-Aboriginal homes (59). Prior to the late 1970s an unknown number of Aboriginal children in Canada were adopted in the United States. By 1980 this practice had been discontinued in all provinces except Manitoba, which reported fifty-four Aboriginal children placed for adoption in the United States. The controversy surrounding this practice initiated a public inquiry, led by Justice Edwin C. Kimmelman, into adoptions and placements of First Nations and Métis children. Justice Kimmelman reported in 1985:

> In 1982, no one except the Indian and Métis people really believed the reality – that Native children were routinely being shipped to adoption homes in the United States and to other provinces in Canada ... No one fully comprehended that 25 percent of all children placed for adoption were placed outside of Manitoba. No one fully comprehended that virtually all those children were of Native descent ... Families approached agencies for help and found that what was described as being in the child's "best interest" resulted in their families being torn asunder and siblings separated ... The road to hell was paved with good intentions, and the child welfare system was the paving contractor. (RCAP 1996, 3:29)

To the Aboriginal peoples of Canada, contact with Canadian child welfare systems has meant the legalized separation of children from families and communities and their placement in Christian residential schools, in white foster homes, and with non-Aboriginal adoptive parents. These actions have been justified by the argument that the child's best interest is being protected.

Interpretations of Aboriginal Peoples' Experience of Canadian Child Welfare

The child welfare literature interprets Aboriginal peoples' experience of Canadian child welfare in three significant ways. First, it is viewed as a consequence of poverty. Within liberal democracies, child welfare intervention occurs disproportionately in relation to the poor (Lindsey 1994; Pelton 1994; Corby 1991; van Krieken 1991; Wharf 1995). As Brian Wharf (1995, 3) notes: "Twenty years ago the National Council on Welfare reported that 'one fundamental characteristic of the child welfare system has not changed appreciably over the years: its clients are still overwhelmingly drawn from the ranks of Canada's poor.'"

Pelton (1994, 17) argues that, "even though most impoverished parents do not abuse or neglect their children, children from impoverished and low-income families are vastly over represented in the incidence of child abuse and neglect. This strong relationship holds not only for child abuse and neglect in general but for every identified form including emotional abuse, emotional neglect and sexual abuse." In Canada the poor are disproportionately First Nations, women, the young, and parents with children (National Council of Welfare 1997).

The second interpretation of Canadian child welfare intervention as it relates to Aboriginal peoples can be viewed as part of the colonization process – the process of subjecting First Nations peoples to the norms and values of the dominant Euro-Canadian culture: "Colonialism involves creating dependency among a nation or group, the objective of which includes the extraction of benefits by the dominant nation or group" (McKenzie and Hudson 1985, 130). McKenzie and Hudson (1985, 130, 131) argue that there are two types of colonialism – structural and cultural:

Structural colonialism involves the explicit control of power and decision-making by the dominant group for the purpose of extracting benefits ... Such benefits today include resource extraction from lands occupied by native people and the utilization of native people as reserve labour and as consumers of goods and services, including social services ... Cultural colonialism involves efforts to achieve normative control of a minority group or culture. These efforts are designed to explain and legitimize actual control, and historical efforts designed to "civilize the savage" reflect this tradition ... A major attribute of the colonial relationship involves the location of power and decision-making structures within the dominant society ... In the child welfare system, policies and procedures have been established in law and executed by courts and agencies with no input from native people. The child welfare system is geographically removed from native communities, and services have been provided primarily by non-native workers who live outside those communities. Decisions related to apprehension and custody, then have been made primarily outside native communities, and these processes have generally continued to deny the existence of formal or informal political and social structures within the local community.

Devaluation is an integral characteristic of the colonial relationship, and it depends on "acceptance of the belief that the colonizer is the sole carrier of a valid culture" (ibid.). In child welfare, this has occurred by individualizing, medicalizing, and legalizing Aboriginal peoples' concerns with childcare. Traditional ways of responding to parental neglect or abuse through community-based intervention have been ignored.

In 1992 the Aboriginal committee reviewing family and children's services legislation in British Columbia echoed these themes in a section of their report entitled "Cultural Genocide":

> The government's goal in creating them [the residential schools] was to separate our people from our culture, and to instill European cultural values in us. This was to be accomplished by creating the greatest possible separation between our children and their extended families, minimizing the opportunities of our cultural values being passed on to our children. (Community Panel 1992, 18)

The committee further noted:

> Prevalent social views in the 1950s and 1960s were that our children, facing the conditions of poverty forced upon our communities, needed protection. The lack of running water in an Aboriginal household was often sufficient excuse for the apprehension of a child ... The "best interests of the child" was and still is, interpreted as rescuing the children from their Aboriginal condition and placing them in a non-Aboriginal environment where they can learn the dominant cultural values. (19)

> Our traditional community-based approaches to resolving problems have been replaced by European medical models of treating individuals in isolation from their social environment. In most cases, this type of treatment has been unsuccessful in solving problems for us ... The failures of this approach have been used to justify the continued apprehension of our children, thereby perpetuating a cycle of cultural confusion. (22)

The objective of colonization is that the dominant group in a society obtains effective power and control over a subordinated group through creating a dependency relationship.

The third interpretation of Canadian child welfare intervention sees it as part of the processes of social regulation within a capitalist society.

This suggests that child welfare's function is to readjust the social institution of the family to conform with emerging systems of corporate capitalism. Initially expressed in the 1970s, this view holds that "child welfare constitutes the assertion of social control by capitalist-inspired, middle-class social pathologists like social workers, psychologists, teachers [and] doctors over the working class family" (van Krieken 1991, 18). Its aim is the production of well disciplined workers who are industrious and self-reliant citizens within a capitalist economy. The child welfare system guaranteed the class structure of capitalism by controlling unruly elements among the working class. Historically, "it was imposed on society by the forces of organized virtue, led by feminists, temperance advocates, educational reformers, liberal ministers, penologists, doctors and bureaucrats" (C. Lasch in van Krieken 1991, 19). "It would not have been capable of achieving significant reforms without the financial and political support of the most powerful and wealthy sectors of society" (A. Platt in van Krieken 1991, 17). Donzelot (1997, 19-21) developed this theme to describe the loss of family autonomy to a "tutelary complex" of policing agencies that view the poor and working class as a "missionary field" in which to apply the knowledge-claims and practices of the new human sciences – medicine, psychiatry, psychology, and criminology. Individuals who present problems are integrated into society through moralization, normalization, and tutelage, and it is through these techniques that the state gains increased surveillance opportunities pertaining to the private life of the family. The techniques of "therapeutism" (Epstein 1994; Berger 1977) are sophisticated means of exercising power. They are "not simply imposed from above in the form of direct constraint or imposition but via encouraging and supporting individuals to exercise their own freedoms and choices, thereby allowing government at a distance" (Parton 1994, 12). The fusion of state power and the human sciences intermeshes welfare and penalty, with the result that social control becomes invisible and the social regulation of the family, community, and other aspects of social life become more pervasive (Parton 1991, 7). According to this interpretation, social work's role can be characterized as one of mediation: "Social work essentially occupies the space between the respectable and the deviant or dangerous classes, and between those with access to political and speaking rights and those who are excluded. It fulfills an essential mediating role between those who are actually or potentially excluded and the mainstream of society" (15).

These arguments continue to exert a significant influence on recent analyses of child welfare (van Krieken 1991, 21; Parton 1991). The development of critical social work practice theories (Mulally 2002; Mulally 1997; Carniol 2000; Pease and Fook 1999; Payne 1997) suggests that social workers may be able to undertake an analysis of the oppressive features of class, race, gender, and ability within a child protection practice situation. This may enable them to take a progressive approach to intervention. However, there is little empirical knowledge regarding the ideas that actually inform social workers' protection practice as it pertains to Aboriginal children, families, and communities.

In general, the prominent interpretive themes found in the child welfare literature – poverty, colonization, and social regulation – do not focus specific attention on the nature of child welfare policy or social work practice with regard to child protection. Whether social work practice is a function of colonial and class relationships circumscribed by the regulatory framework, or whether there is a measure of independent analysis, reflection, and judgment on the part of the practitioner is unclear. Critical social work practice theories suggest there should be independent analysis and reflection, but there is little evidence to show that this occurs in practice (Barsky, Rogers, Krysik, and Langevin 1997; Carew 1979, 361-62; Payne 1997, 46-7).

3
The British Columbia Context

Between the mid-1950s and the early 1970s large numbers of Aboriginal children entered the BC child welfare system for the first time. In 1955 only twenty-nine Indian children were in the care of the BC superintendent of child welfare. By 1960 this number had risen to 849, and in 1964 it had risen to 1,446. In a period of ten years Aboriginal children shifted from under 1 percent of the total children in care in British Columbia to about 32 percent. The rate fluctuated between 36.7 percent and 39.2 percent from 1976 to 1980 (Stanbury 1975, 384; Johnston 1983, 27). The rapid increase of Aboriginal children in the BC child welfare system can be explained by the federal policy of integration, the extension of child welfare laws to reserves, and the liberalization of liquor laws, all of which occurred in the early 1950s.

A number of amendments were made to the Indian Act in 1951, following the 1948 *Report of the Special Joint Committee of the Senate and the House of Commons on the Indian Act.* Education was the major focus of the Special Joint Committee's work, and integration of Aboriginal peoples into mainstream society became the theme of Canadian government policy. Educating Aboriginal children "for citizenship" with children from different backgrounds in common classrooms became the priority. It was no longer considered to be acceptable to racially segregate children in separate schools. This policy enabled Ottawa to avoid capital expenditures on new schools and to rely on the provinces and local school boards to provide classrooms for Aboriginal students. Money would be saved by not duplicating school buildings, and, at the same time, responsibility for the quality of instruction would be shifted to the provinces (Miller 1996, 383). The emphasis on integration was advocated by some Aboriginal leaders and communities in the hope that their children would receive a better education in provincial schools than they would in residential schools or band schools (K. Wasacase, personal communication, 21 September 1999). Integration policy was also attractive because, for the first time, it enabled the Department of Indian Affairs to provide secondary school education to Aboriginal children without the capital expenditure of constructing new schools. Aboriginal children were integrated into provincial schools in or close to their home communities, and they came increasingly within the orbit of provincial law. As this occurred, residential schools assumed a residual function as residences for children attending provincial schools from isolated communities; sometimes they served as a placement resource for orphaned or abandoned children.

The 1951 amendments to the Indian Act included a new Section 88. According to Indian affairs officials, this provided the legal authority to extend child welfare services to all Aboriginal children in a province, including those on reserves (MacDonald 1993, 19). In 1952 the Provincial Welfare Branch began providing services to Aboriginal people in "matters relative to delinquent children, unmarried mothers and adoption cases" (Stanbury 1975, 210). A 1955 policy permitting the apprehension of Indian children on-reserve initiated a trend towards the removal of Aboriginal children from their families and communities.

Between 1951 and 1956 the discriminatory provisions of the Indian Act, along with BC laws concerning the possession, purchase, and consumption of alcohol by Aboriginal people, were removed. This liberalization, argued for on the grounds of social equality and non-discrimination, was based in a belief that "Indians should be permitted to drink in the open." There also appeared to be a dimension of political necessity involved as status Indians were given the right to vote in BC provincial elections in 1951. These changes were advocated by some Aboriginal leaders but were hotly contested by others (Hawthorn, Belshaw, and Jamieson 1958, 378, 382). Prior to 1951 Aboriginal people were not permitted to purchase liquor at liquor stores, take liquor onto reserves, or consume liquor in a public place. British Columbia amended its laws in 1951 to give Aboriginal people "access to beer parlours and licensed establishments serving meals" (378). By 1955 an amendment to the Indian Act was passed to permit Aboriginal people to drink off-reserve if such activity was permitted by the laws of the province. In 1956 the federal government granted full liquor rights to Aboriginal peoples (378).

For the first time Aboriginal people could drink at home, in restaurants, and at social gatherings without fear of legal consequences. But the removal of a century's worth of restrictions in the space of a few years had dramatic effects. Hawthorn argued that, in the previous prohibition period, a social pattern of "wild and secretive" drinking had been established; but with secrecy no longer required, drinking to excess came into the open (Hawthorn, Belshaw, and Jamieson 1958, 381). In a study for the *Royal Commission on Aboriginal Peoples* a member of the Spallumcheen Band made the following observation:

> These changes in liquor policies of governments encouraged and led to excessive drinking among our Band members, both on the reserve and in the adjoining towns of Enderby and Armstrong. Our Elder Romeo Edwards recalls the period of the next ten years as a time when "everything went crazy" and when "drinking affected every household." He notes that people began drinking who had never touched liquor before in their lives. It became a regular social activity and way of life affecting both the old and the young. It led to many deaths from violence, suicides, accidents, and impaired health ... [and] caused Band members to lose respect for themselves and one another ... [and created] a weakened sense of responsibility for the care of children and family members. (MacDonald 1993, 18, 19)

During the late 1950s and early 1960s Aboriginal children's integration into provincial child welfare services occurred at an alarming velocity, but the first Department of Social Welfare policy directive about status Indian children did not appear until 1966. It advised that planning for status Indian children was "the sole responsibility of the Department of Social Welfare," that "every effort should be made to find a suitable placement with an Indian family," and that admission to a residential school should be discouraged unless there was proper guardianship (Department of Social Welfare 1966, 2.09). This period, referred to as the sixties scoop, has not been the subject of any systematic research focusing on how social workers or the department thought about practice. As one social worker observed, "provincial social workers would, quite literally, scoop children from reserves on the slightest pretext, because they believed that what they were doing was in the best interests of the child ... They felt that the apprehension of Indian children from reserves would save them from the effects of crushing poverty, unsanitary health conditions, poor housing, and malnutrition" (Johnston 1983, 23). However, during this same period another social worker (at the Vancouver Children's Aid Society) reports that they did make efforts to place children in Aboriginal homes, although few such resources were available. They also considered the child's relationship to the family, but whether the detrimental effects of separation from the

extended family and community were considered is unclear (C. Corn-
wall, personal communication, 29 October 1999).

In spite of significant change to the BC child-in-care caseload that
began in 1955 and accelerated through the 1960s, there was no research
on the phenomenon until 1974. First, a small study by the Union of BC
Indian Chiefs for the BC Ministry of Human Resources outlined adoption and other child welfare issues. Then W.T. Stanbury, a member of
the Faculty of Commerce and Business Administration at UBC, published *Success and Failure: Indians in Urban Society.* This was the first study
thoroughly to report the dimensions of the change. Published with a
grant from the BC Departments of Labour and Human Resources, it
found that the number of children of Indian racial origin in government care grew from 1,100 in 1962 to 2,825 in 1973, an increase of 157
percent in eleven years. By comparison, the total number of children in
care increased only 82 percent. In 1972 Indian children comprised 5
percent of the province's child population but 27 percent of the child
population in government care (Stanbury 1975, 210-11). Between 1976
and 1979 Aboriginal children made up approximately 27 percent of the
children placed for adoption and about 44 percent of the children in
foster homes (Johnston 1983). Despite this dramatic social change, it
was not until 1980 that the BC government's removal of Aboriginal
children from families and communities became a political issue.

NDP Government Reforms
With the election of the New Democratic Party (NDP) government of
Dave Barrett in 1972, a new era of social policy reform began. Juvenile
jails were closed and the use of the strap to discipline children in BC
schools was banned. The Family and Children's Law Commission was
appointed in 1973 under the leadership of Justice Thomas Berger. In
nineteen months it produced thirteen reports, a draft children's statute,
and a unified family court project (Cruickshank 1985, 182). The tenth
report of the commission, *Native Families and the Law,* resulted from
eight conferences held throughout the province with 260 Aboriginal
representatives. It found that most reserve communities did not provide
their own child welfare services and that the provincial services provided on-reserve were confused and haphazard, were limited to crisis
situations, and had little concern with prevention (British Columbia
1974, 4). The commission found "some social workers dominate Indian
communities so much that the Indians no longer feel it worthwhile to
protest the frequent removal of children from homes" (6). It also found
very few Aboriginal social workers – only fourteen Aboriginal graduates

of college welfare aide programs, six Aboriginal registered social workers, and fewer than one master of social work graduate per year. The commission also observed that adoption practice in North America was strongly influenced by the "widespread conviction that native children placed in non-Indian adoption homes would suffer no ill effects, if the homes were loving and supportive" (26). The commission noted that there were a disproportionate number of Aboriginal children available for adoption in British Columbia, along with a lack of success in recruiting Aboriginal adoption homes.

The Berger Commission proposed forty-one wide-ranging recommendations encompassing three themes: (1) the increased cultural awareness of non-Aboriginal professionals, (2) the increased participation and representation of Aboriginal persons in human service decision making, and (3) the increased preservation of Aboriginal children's cultural heritage. It recommended that Indian custom adoptions be legalized and that subsidies "be available as needed" to enable Aboriginal adoption of Aboriginal children.[1] It also recommended, for the first time, that an Aboriginal child's home community be notified when that child was taken into care. In spite of the ground-breaking work of the commission, it was not until the 1990s that many of its recommendations were implemented.

The 1981 Family and Child Service Act and the Beginning of Aboriginal Child Welfare Services

In 1978 the BC government announced its intention to revise the province's child welfare legislation and released a white paper for public comment. Legislation had not been extensively revised since 1939, although an amendment was passed in 1967 to make reporting of child abuse mandatory. The major modifications proposed to the 1939 act were: to repeal provisions dealing with unmanageability; to provide for short-term custody agreements for the first time, which included agreements for mentally and physically disabled children; to expand protection jurisdiction to nineteen years from seventeen; to introduce provisions for confidentiality; and to introduce measures to deal with emergency situations (Callahan and Wharf 1982, 51). However, unlike the situation in many Canadian provinces at the time, there was no recognition of emotional neglect, no legislative requirement to provide family support or prevention services, and no right for the child to be

---

[1] Indian custom adoptions occur when a family or community member raises a child as their own.

consulted prior to a protection hearing or judicial decision. In general, the legislation failed to incorporate the central recommendations of the Berger Commission on children's rights and provided no recognition of the special needs of Aboriginal communities. The new legislation was severely criticized by BC child welfare professionals, both in draft stages and in its final form. Its narrow legislative focus and emphasis on child removal was in sharp contrast to the Berger Commission's emphasis on prevention, family support, children's rights, and lay/community involvement in decision making (Durie and Armitage 1995, 3).

Perhaps coincidental with the new child welfare legislation, or because of a growing awareness of community devastation, Spallumcheen became the first BC Aboriginal community to take control of child welfare policy and services (MacDonald 1985). Between 1962 and 1966 seventy-five of approximately 155 Spallumcheen children had been removed from the community. By the late 1970s many of these young people were returning to the reserve after running away from a foster home or reaching the age of majority. "A good proportion of these returnees had become addicted to alcohol or drugs and at least eleven of them met with a violent death from accidents, suicide, or homicide within two years" (MacDonald 1993, 24). By the late 1970s the Spallumcheen Band was determined to face the family and youth problems of its community. In 1979 Wayne Christian, an adult survivor of the child welfare system, was elected chief of the Spallumcheen Band. After being approached by a mother whose four children had been removed by the BC Ministry of Human Resources, Christian brought the issue before the band council. The band drafted a child welfare by-law in early 1980 and proposed it to the minister of Indian affairs, the Honorable John Munro. The minister at first disallowed the by-law as unconstitutional since it permitted a band to exercise child welfare powers, which were the exclusive jurisdiction of the province. After minor changes and intense lobbying, the minister agreed to the by-law, which came into effect on 3 September 1980. The band then turned its attention towards the BC government. The minister of human resources, Grace McCarthy, was urged to respect the powers conferred on the band by the new child welfare by-law. After a motorized caravan of Aboriginal people to Vancouver, a march of over 1,000 persons through the city's streets, and a rally outside the minister's fashionable Vancouver home, she agreed to a meeting. The next day a handwritten agreement resulted from a lengthy meeting with the minister. She agreed "to respect the authority of the Spallumcheen Band Council to assume authority and control over their children" and "to the desirability of returning Indian children of the Spallumcheen Band presently in the care of the Minister to the authority of the Spallumcheen Band" (MacDonald 1993, 28). By the spring of 1981 the Spallumcheen child welfare program was in operation, and plans were developed to return about twenty-five Spallumcheen children still in the care of the ministry. The Spallumcheen by-law empowers the chief, band councillors, and persons authorized by them to remove a child of the band believed to be in need of protection. It requires the child to be brought before chief and council within seven days and authorizes them to make a decision on placement, guided by "Indian" customs and preferences and the wishes of the child. It also provides a rank-ordered list of preferred resources for the child, beginning with a member of her/his immediate family and moving to an extended family member, an Indian on-reserve, an Indian off-reserve, and, as a last resort, a non-Indian off-reserve (MacDonald 1993, 31). The Spallumcheen Band's child welfare bylaw is an achievement that has not been attained by any other band in Canada.

Perhaps related to the Spallumcheen controversy, or as a consequence of the implementation of the new Child and Family Services Act, the Ministry of Human Resources revised its child protection policy for Status Indian children in 1981, the first such revision since 1966. The new policy stated that, when a Status Indian child was likely to be removed, social workers should notify the band and encourage the band's participation in planning for the child. In addition, the social worker should discuss with the parent(s) all possible resources available to them, including the extended family (MHR, *Policy and Procedures Manual* 1981, 2.9.16).

In 1981 the Nuu-Chah-Nulth Tribal Council began a process to take control of child welfare services in its community. Like the Spallumcheen Band it was very concerned about the increasing number of its children entering the provincial child welfare system. In 1983 it initiated a community development process to prepare communities for the takeover of child welfare services. The tribal council negotiated with the provincial government in order to obtain the delegated authority of the superintendent of child welfare, and it negotiated with the federal government in order to obtain a five-year funding agreement. The Usma program was phased in during 1987, and by 1988 it was fully operational. It provides child protection, substitute care, reunification services, infant development, community services, and cultural programs to members of fourteen bands located on the west coast of Vancouver Island (Usma Nuu-Chah-Nulth Family and Child Services Program 1999).

During the late 1980s pressure for reform of the BC child welfare system was building. There were increasing rates of family poverty, unemployment, single-parent and blended families, teenage pregnancy, youth homelessness, prostitution, and drug abuse. In addition, there was new public awareness of sexual abuse, foetal alcohol syndrome, and drug use. As awareness of the number of Aboriginal children in care increased and the self-government movement gained momentum, pressure for Aboriginal control of child welfare services also mounted. All provinces except Newfoundland and the Northwest Territories amended their child welfare legislation during the 1980s. In British Columbia advocates of family preservation argued that prevention and family support were the most effective means of protecting children. In 1990 the BC ombudsman released a report on the need for advocacy, service integration, uniform standards of care, and procedural safeguards in relation to a child's death at the Eagle Rock Youth Ranch in 1989. At the invitation of the Ministry of Social Services, the ombudsman prepared a second report in 1991 to summarize recommended legislative changes. By the time this report was released, a legislative review was under way.

The 1990s: Decade of Reform
An NDP government was again elected in British Columbia on 17 October 1991 under the leadership of Michael Harcourt, and Joan Smallwood was appointed minister of social services and housing. This initiated an ongoing series of reform processes throughout the rest of the decade, concurrent with the NDP's two electoral mandates: (1) community consultations, new legislation, and a judicial inquiry and (2) a reorganization of the service delivery system. In November 1991 the minister announced the formation of two community panels, one Aboriginal and one non-Aboriginal, to hold public meetings and to receive submissions concerning child welfare legislation and services. The minister released the reports of the community panels to the public on 3 December 1992 and announced a moratorium on the adoption of Aboriginal children to non-Aboriginal homes as well as the planned appointment of British Columbia's first Aboriginal deputy superintendent of child welfare (Durie and Armitage 1995, 23). The Community Panel reports addressed broad systemic issues in child welfare and made specific proposals for child protection, youth services, children in care, adoption, and dispute resolution.

The Aboriginal Panel Report stressed that First Nations law and traditions entail a holistic view of nature and human relationships and do not view children as the possessions of parents. The report stated that what was needed was a recognition of the inherent right to self-government, culturally appropriate child welfare, and adequate resources for the implementation of preventive services and family support services. In September 1993 a major Cabinet shuffle occurred, and Joy MacPhail became minister of social services. Planning proceeded to introduce new child welfare legislation in the spring 1994 session of the Legislature. However, in the spring of 1994 the public became aware of the death of five-year-old Matthew Vaudreuil, who, throughout his life, had been a client of the Ministry of Social Services. The day before new legislation was introduced in the Legislature, the minister announced an independent inquiry led by Judge Thomas Gove of the BC Provincial Court. He was appointed to "inquire, report, and make recommendations on the adequacy of services and the policies and practices of the Ministry of Social Services as they relate to the death of Matthew Vaudreuil" (Durie and Armitage 1995, 36). The Child, Family, and Community Services Act and the Child, Youth, and Family Advocacy Act were passed in the Legislature on 20 and 21 June 1994, respectively. However, the introduction and passage of new legislation at the same time as the announcement of a judicial inquiry created confusion about the direction of the reform process.

The Gove Report's release in November 1995 unleashed a new wave of reform processes in British Columbia's child and family services. These focused on administrative procedure, professional education, service integration, and the internal and external review of practice. The structural issues emphasized in the Community Panel Reports, such as poverty and self-government, were left untouched, and preventive services as well as family and community involvement were set aside. The new legislation, proclaimed in January 1996, left unproclaimed most of the progressive features of the act, such as the sections on family conferences, service agreements with a child's kin, and youth services (Durie and Armitage 1995, 5). These were not implemented until 1999 (youth services) and 2002 (family conferences, service agreements with a child's kin), respectively.

From the point of view of Aboriginal child welfare, the Child, Family, and Community Services Act is significant because it introduces, for the first time, a legislative principle that holds that Aboriginal heritage should be preserved and that Aboriginal communities have the right to participate in child welfare decision making. It also recognizes that the child's family is the preferred environment for the child. Passed at the same time, the Child, Youth, and Family Advocacy Act established an independent system of advocacy for children entitled to receive services under the Child, Family, and Community Services Act. However, the new legislation limits family support to "available services" and is non-specific about what community involvement or cultural heritage means in practice.

The province's first child, youth and family advocate, Joyce Preston, was sworn into office on 15 May 1995. Her first annual report, and each subsequent report, addressed concerns about Aboriginal children. In 1995 she observed that Aboriginal children and youth in care "are growing up in great uncertainty and sometimes [are] being left in limbo" due to treaty negotiations, the moratorium on the adoption of Aboriginal children and youth by non-Aboriginal families, and the development of Aboriginal self-government (Office of the Child, Youth, and Family Advocate 1995, 13). In 1997 she reported that 35 percent of the children in government care were Aboriginal and that the concerns she had raised in her 1995 *Annual Report* still existed. Although the Ministry of Children and Family Development developed a draft strategic plan for Aboriginal Services in 1997, the advocate was concerned that "today's children and youth may well be grown up before the various governments involved have fully developed these services" (Office of the Child, Youth, and Family Advocate 1997, 62). She indicated plans to create an advocate for Aboriginal services in the next fiscal year. However, following the election of the Liberal government of Premier Gordon Campbell in 2001, the Advocate's Office was eliminated and its legislation repealed.

In March 1996 the Ministry of Children and Family Development created an Aboriginal Relations Branch and Policy Division to provide support and direction to Aboriginal groups in the province who wished to provide statutory child welfare services to their communities. Preceding the creation of this branch, and continuing after its initiation, a series of delegated authority agreements was developed with bands and tribal councils in the province. These are summarized in Table 2.

The twenty approved agreements for the provision of child protection services cover approximately 50 percent of the 200 bands in British Columbia. These agreements include a Métis organization in the South Fraser region of Greater Vancouver and an urban child welfare organization in Vancouver/Richmond. An additional forty bands are planning the development of an Aboriginal child welfare organization at this time (BC Ministry of Children and Family Development 2004).

In late 1996 the Ministry of Children and Family Development began a major reorganization in order to implement Judge Gove's recommendation of an integrated service delivery system. This involved integrating, into one ministry, children's mental health, youth probation, drug

Table 2

Delegated authority agreements between the director of child welfare and Aboriginal organizations in BC for the provision of child welfare services to Aboriginal children and families

12 November 1987	Usma Nuu-Chah-Nulth Community and Human Services
22 January 1993	Lalum'utul' Smun'een Child and Family Services (Cowichan Indian Band)
28 April 1993	Sechelt Child and Family Services
28 April 1993	Ayas Men Men Child and Family Services (Squamish Indian Band)
31 May 1994	Scw'exmx Child and Family Services (Nicola Valley Tribal Council)
22 September 1994	Nlha'7kapmx Child and Family Services
26 November 1993	Sto:lo Health and Family Services
13 October 1995	Knucwentwecw Society (Cariboo Tribal Council)
5 May 1997	Nisga'a Family and Child Services
8 December 1997	Kwumut Lelum Central Island Child and Family Services Society
29 January 1998	Carrier-Sekani Family Services
8 February 1999	Northwest Internation Family Services Society
5 March 1999	Nil/Tu'o Child and Family Services
3 June 1999	Gitxsan Child and Family Services
27 July 1999	Ktunaxa-Kinbasket Family and Child Services
6 March 2000	Secwepemc Child and Family Services
31 March 2000	Heiltsuk Kaxla Child and Family Service Program
11 April 2001	Metis Family Services
20 September 2001	Vancouver Aboriginal Child and Family Services Society
31 July 2002	Nezul Be Hunuyeh Child and Family Services

Source: BC Ministry of Children and Family Development (2004).

and alcohol services for youth, child protection, guardianship, community living, and family support services. However, this reorganization accentuated an ongoing morale and staffing crisis. On 5 March 1997, six months after the reorganization process began, about 175 social workers demonstrated outside the Vancouver constituency office of Premier Glen Clark as well as outside of other MLA's offices throughout the province. The protest was organized "to demonstrate the serious shortage of social workers and the bureaucratic changes that are stealing time away from the front-line" (*Vancouver Sun* 1997, A1). The social workers argued that increased paperwork was forcing them to spend less time with families and more time "behind a desk," thereby creating an impossible workload.

Six months later, a *Vancouver Sun* column by Paula Brook (1997a) on the "rush to re-organization" triggered an outpouring of concern from social workers, unlike anything the journalist had experienced. Her voice mail was filled with messages from social workers. One social worker noted that work with high-risk families is stressful but that it is nothing compared to being treated as worthless by one's employer: "You take on all this responsibility for a system that is inept to begin with and then it gets worse and continues to get worse, and you are rewarded by being blamed publicly for not doing your job, and pilloried by the press every time a child falls through one of the enormous cracks that are endemic to the system" (Brook 1997b, A21).

By summer 1998 the *Vancouver Province* reported social workers re-signing or retiring from the "job from hell" at an alarming rate. The BC Government Employees Union indicated that social workers had signed 200 statements advising they were unable to maintain minimum child protection standards and that one in ten employees had requested em-ployee-assistance help for work-related difficulties (Tait 1998, 11). A ministry-union study completed in 1997 showed that staffing levels were far below an acceptable standard. Social workers frequently re-ported caseloads above fifty, whereas the Child Welfare League of America recommends a caseload of twenty. The ministry's difficulty in attract-ing and retaining staff when combined with the number and complex-ity of changes implemented since 1996 had created an ongoing morale crisis. In the following chapters I explore practitioners' thinking about the effects these changes have had on practice, on the ministry's rela-tionship with Aboriginal communities, and on the welfare of Aborigi-nal children.

4
A Description of Practice

I never thought I would do child protection.

– A non-Aboriginal social worker employed
in an Aboriginal organization

This chapter describes the everyday work of child protection from the practitioner's point of view. It begins by explaining how social workers enter the field of child protection and then goes on to discuss how practitioners "think on their feet," ensure safety in dangerous conditions, build relationships with families, manage stress, deal with isolation in small communities, respond to the sense of being watched, engage in complex decision making, and find satisfaction in their work.

Getting into Child Protection
The entry point to child protection practice is usually a social work degree and a child welfare practicum. But for Aboriginal and non-Aboriginal practitioners, respectively, there are significant differences in experience, and these inform their practice entry. For many, entry to child protection was accidental or serendipitous, with the first contact not necessarily being positive. As one social worker indicated: "the practicum was my first actual thing of child protection and it wasn't like a positive one. Like they were helpful and cooperative, but looking at where they were standing from their caseloads ... most people would have gone into another field."

The conditions of practice appeared daunting, but the support this practitioner received at her practicum seemed to make the difference in the decision to begin a child protection career. One Aboriginal practitioner saw working in child protection as a "total error": "I never saw myself working in the area of child welfare ... I took the BSW program at [university] and graduated from that and did my practicum with my band and the practicum was with a child welfare program ... and they offered me the position after the practicum was over and so, not realizing what I was getting into I guess, accepted and the rest is all history."

A Ministry of Children and Family Development (MCFD) practitioner conveys a sense of entrapment: "I got in and I couldn't get out ... I did my practicum in the ___ office, and from there I just got hired and never left." Many had not thought about child welfare as a career choice, but the prospect of a job became sufficient motivation: "I didn't pick child welfare specifically; I knew I just wanted to work in the field of social work and it happened that that is where I got my start. I enjoyed it and it went from there." Only one practitioner indicated an intention to enter the field prior to a university field practicum in social work: "Going to university was always my first choice. I always wanted to be involved in child protection."

Non-Aboriginal social workers explain their entry into child protection by referring to the availability of work and accidental circumstances. Some express incredulity that they are actually doing child protection. The contrast between their previous thinking and their present work suggests that, before their entry into the field, it was not uncommon for many of them to find child protection practice distasteful. More than one boldly stated: "I never thought I would do child protection."

By contrast, Aboriginal practitioners describe their entry into child protection work as complex and intentional. Some hope to contribute to their community's welfare. An Aboriginal practitioner at MCFD wanted to go back to her band with more understanding of the ministry system. Another, employed by an Aboriginal organization, wanted to be able "to help out in the community." The decision to become a child protection practitioner often evolves out of personal and family experiences with child protection. An Aboriginal social worker at MCFD described a variety of social workers in her life. She decided to become a social worker when she was a preteen as she believed that she could do a better job than some she encountered. Another had a strong motivation to "do some good" with regard to sexual abuse because she had been sexually abused as a child. Another's interest in child protection developed from the responsibilities she had for the younger members of her family:

I basically took care of my younger siblings when my parents were off drinking and partying and trying to keep them away from them and from possible abuse ... Same thing with my cousins, there is one that is a year younger than me, and she was in the same position as well, so we kind of took care of all the younger ones and you know, sometimes it would be between six and ten of us, kind of keeping each other safe.

Most Aboriginal practitioners have had experience with child protection in their family and community before beginning professional practice. One remembers her father's contact with the system:

My parents ended up separating so my dad raised me on his own, being a single parent, I guess the ministry decided that it wouldn't be a good thing for a single man to raise a daughter so, my dad told me this one story actually where a social worker came up to check on the situation, decided that a single parent man couldn't raise a daughter, and said "Well, we have to take her out of the home." My dad, I guess, became somewhat threatening and I was sure [he was] somewhat verbally reprimanding – whatever word you want to use – and said, "You're not taking her," and she said, "Well, I'll be back up with the RCMP, Mr. ___," and he said, "Well you go right ahead. My shotgun will be waiting for you." And I guess the social worker never came back.

Another remembered her grandfather's intervention and how it prevented her from entering the child protection system. Aboriginal practitioners have vivid memories of child protection practices that non-Aboriginal practitioners do not, and this motivates them differently than non-Aboriginal practitioners. There is a personal experience base and desire "to make a difference" among Aboriginal practitioners that is not evident among non-Aboriginal practitioners.

Non-Aboriginal practitioners generally had little contact with the child protection system before beginning professional practice: "I remember going to see friends as a teen who lived up in northern Alberta and them talking about foster kids in their home and me not knowing – what is that?" Another offers the following memory:

On our street, in our neighbourhood, across the road this family fostered. So we had lots of foster kids in our neighbourhood. And we couldn't figure out why this particular family ... had all these kids and they kept changing and then we realized that they were foster kids, but we didn't understand what foster children were. It's just that when we played street hockey or whatever, it was just different kids playing.

The memories of non-Aboriginal practitioners are distant, remote, and outside their families' experience.

Practitioners Describing Practice

"Varied," "exciting," "frustrating," "demanding," "stressful," "a learning process," "isolating," "fascinating," "painful," "creative," "hectic," "challenging," and "interesting" are words social workers use to describe their practice. To some employed at the BC MCFD, there is an "adrenaline rush" that comes with the work: "it's almost an A type personality [that] has to be attracted to child protection because it's adrenaline rush, it's thinking on your feet, it's immediate decision making, it's calling into play all your resources, your facilities, your training, your skill to make decisions at a certain point in time." One regards it as addictive: "There's sort of an adrenaline fix to it that occurs."

In rural communities, "instead of being trapped in an office all the time," workers have a sense of freedom and adventure, which comes with their required travel: "it was great ... flying four hundred miles up the trench in a helicopter, coming down on a trapline just to serve somebody some court papers, and try[ing] to locate them in the bush and really getting to know people, you know. We'd get snowed in on some of these places and have to spend the nights, and you know it was a real sense of adventure and fun." But child protection is also unpredictable, demanding flexibility and adaptability and an ongoing ability to "think on your feet." One social worker in an isolated community described her work as follows:

> In the communities you are working by yourself so you have to de-velop a lot of skills. You don't have the support here so you're just there and you have to think on your feet ... Every time you go in to do an investigation, you've got to think, okay, you've got to plan where you're going to, who you're going to talk to first, how you're going to coordinate it, what's your decision going to be. How can I calm this person down if they're very upset? You have a limited time if you're doing interviews at the school. You've got to get back over to the community and there isn't a boat there to take you over and it's like, how can I coordinate everything? And am I making the right decision by removing?

In an isolated community, you are "constantly trying to improvise" to create adequate services for a family because the services "just aren't there." According to a male practitioner in an MCFD after-hours service:

There's been times like I've had to do things at night that are incredible
and that's part of the fun of the job – coming to a house, call on some
intoxicated parents and knocking at the door and the kids, 4, 5, 6 an-
swering the door and saying, "Mom's sleeping on the couch," and me
asking them to go wake her up and them not being able to and just
taking legal authority to go into the house and try and wake her and
not being able to and having to take the kids and put them in the car,
and call somebody about this parent, her waking up after a period of
time, but still being fairly inebriated but very upset and, you know,
threatening my life, and all sorts of things.

Child protection demands out-of-the-office work and irregular hours,
and this can be dangerous. Investigations are often conducted at the
child's home or school and may require travel to an isolated area or a
visit to a reserve community. To the non-Aboriginal social worker this
travel amounts to a journey across a cultural boundary. Before leaving
the office, there may be little information about the circumstances to
be encountered, and the worker may have no way of predicting the
family's and community's response. The entire process is imbued with
uncertainty. As one practitioner observes, "It's a vast unknown that you're
walking into."

The ambiguity and uncertainty of child protection leads to different
views about personal safety. Some social workers rarely felt unsafe, others
indicated that they never felt unsafe, and one was "always amazed at
the kindly reception ... that we do get." However, some workers did
feel unsafe, and they did not hesitate to say so. When asked about
whether he ever felt unsafe, one male MCFD practitioner said, "Oh,
many, many, many times." There is no apparent pattern as Aboriginal
and non-Aboriginal practitioners, men and women, supervisors and
front-line workers, highly experienced and not highly experienced are
found in each grouping.

The lack of personal safety that some feel in child protection arises
from the fact that they face potentially dangerous situations. The intrusive nature of an investigation can provoke an angry response from a
child's parents or family members:

I've had it happen where I've showed up on the doorstep and I've had
people yelling and screaming and swearing at you and threatening you,
but I don't get real intimidated by that because I know they're not angry
at me ... It's because you're there and they don't want you to be there.
They're upset because how dare you talk to their kids; you have no right

to interview their child at school, that is one real example. That's happened to me dozens of times, and, you know, and you just deal with it as best as you can, and when that happens you just tell them what you have to tell them and offer to meet with them at the office.

The presence of alcohol can signal danger: "If you know of a family's history, you know there is alcohol – and there is a lot of alcoholism around here – I would either just take a cop with me or get someone else to come with me ... people aren't themselves when they are drunk. I have seen some really nice mellow people that are just ugly, you know. They would never do or say some of the things they have when they are drunk."

The possession of firearms can also be a sign of potential violence. Guns are common in rural communities, and if they are in the hands of an angry family member, then violence is possible: "Everybody has a gun and everybody knows how to use a gun and lots of times disputes were settled and guns were involved within the communities, between each other ... so you do have a sense of not being safe sometimes because of that."

Although the interplay between the intrusive nature of child protection investigations, anger, alcohol, and firearms suggests dangerous conditions for practitioners, in reality few have experienced violence. One MCFD practitioner with over twenty-five years' practice experience observed: "There is only one occasion in which I was actually physically threatened and chased away by an irate parent, and in hindsight, my sympathies are with the parent. I think I handled it very poorly, myself." Only one practitioner, an Aboriginal woman, experienced a violent attack when she was the supervisor of an Aboriginal child welfare program. She describes the situation this way:

> Their children were apprehended and put into ministry care, and they were quite upset with us, and everything kind of just happened so fast and we'd tried numerous interventions with them ... offered them support programs, nothing seemed to work as far as them being able to accept resources and they were quite upset about it, so they came to the band office and I guess they were hollering at one of my caseworkers or something ... all of a sudden they ... barged into my office and started yelling and the next thing I knew, the client, one of the clients was on top of me hitting me in the head, and the male in the situation, who was Native, threatened to put a bullet through my head for them thinking that I was responsible, totally responsible for the removal of their children ... I was hospitalized for a short time after the incident.

Although the occurrence of actual violence in child protection practice appears to be uncommon, its potential is omnipresent. Faced with this condition, practitioners respond differently. Some recognize their fear and live with it. As a female social worker employed by MCFD observed: "I'm not embarrassed to say that I was frightened ... it hasn't been severe enough to report it to the RCMP, no one has stalked my children ... no one has stalked me ... I have gotten a few threatening phone calls, but nothing serious enough to report to the RCMP."

Others denied it: "I'm too stupid, I don't pick up on it; I've been told I'm a dare-devil." However, others recognized that verbal threats and abuse are part of their professional reality, and they learned to live with it. A non-Aboriginal MCFD practitioner commented: "There's been a lot of things that were said. A lot of racial things said, you know, so that didn't bother me. You had to put that into context. You're taking away somebody's child, it's a pretty traumatic thing to do, and so I kind of always expect reactions from people."

Sometimes verbal abuse has political overtones. A non-Aboriginal female practitioner described a recent practice situation:

He's a dad that wasn't too pleased about me being there. He was quite irate and he was very political. He was a Native man, and he was ... making a lot of political statements, not just about me as a social worker, but actually about the band itself because the band social worker was with me as well ... I don't know if he actually scared me, but I just kept my mouth shut for a while and let him rant and rave and then he calmed down enough for us to talk and by the end of our visit, which lasted about an hour, he was very apologetic.

Verbal threats, alcohol, knives, and guns were most frequently mentioned as potential sources of danger, but one social worker mentioned dogs: "Dogs scare me. I had to walk up a driveway once that was really mucky and I remember thinking I am going to get stuck in the mud. I didn't want to take the car. These stupid, two big dogs came running out at me and I thought, what the heck am I going to do now? Thank God they were nice once they reached me." Verbal threats seemed to be the most common danger in Aboriginal communities. According to one Aboriginal MCFD practitioner: "There's a lot of verbal abuse. The women are really verbally aggressive ... they settle their conflicts with violence ... I have been threatened, you know, like when I went to remove a child [and] ... she says, 'You're not taking my child.' And [then she] said, 'If you do that I'll slash your throat.' And she came at me, but she didn't, like she rethought it, I guess ... she had a second thought when she came at me. And [it's] the same with the other people who have grabbed me."

A male MCFD practitioner described a similar reality: "I've had things said ... never had a gun in my face – had knives – but not in the Aboriginal community." Threats to personal safety are evident in child protection, but different practitioners respond differently. Either dangerous conditions are less present for some or their notion of danger differs from that of those who feel threatened. Danger and personal threat exist for them, but they do not occupy centre stage in their minds. An Aboriginal practitioner in an Aboriginal organization recollected only one potentially dangerous incident:

> I think in the four years I worked here at ___, there was only one time I felt unsafe, and at that time I visited a home with the band social worker and the band social worker's husband. It was his brother, so I felt, even though there was drinking going on, we would be safe 'cause he knew the band social worker. We got into the home and he welcomed us in. We went in the kitchen and when we mentioned about the drinking that was going on – it was a party going on and the children being in the home, trying to sleep, going to school the next morning, we felt that the children should not be in the home at this time, that maybe the kids can go with their auntie for the night and we will meet with them tomorrow. He got really upset, and I noticed in the kitchen there was some knives, and I felt a little unsafe at that time ... we left that home, the two boys that were there, they went with their auntie and we got him to a point where he settled down and we were going to meet with him the next day. That was the only time that I felt unsafe.

This encounter appears to have had a minimal impact on this social worker and her practice. However, if she had been non-Aboriginal and without knowledge of the community, would her notion of danger be different? This raises questions as to whether it is the practitioner, the context, or the interaction between the two that informs the worker's notion of danger.

Mediating Danger

Anger, threats, verbal abuse, and violence are possible responses when one knocks on the door to begin an investigation, but some believe the social worker plays a role in creating or mitigating the response received.

According to one MCFD supervisor, "It's very much in the approach that staff take to clients that causes the danger and the non-danger. Now I am not going to say that there are not times when it can't be dangerous, particularly with people who may be under the influence of ... alcohol or cocaine ... it's very much in the way you approach the situation and the words you choose to use with clients in describing why you are there."

Another MCFD practitioner put it this way: "I think too, that if you expect it to happen, it's going to happen more than if you don't ... I've seen social workers walk into situations where they expected something was going to happen, and something did. I walk in, thinking okay, well, it could happen, but it's not gonna and I've not very often had too many problems. I've never been hurt or injured."

The sense of danger accompanying child protection practice may be exaggerated at night: "Whether it is because it is dark and you can't see as well, or whether it is outside of the normal working hours or perhaps your energy level is lower at night, whatever the situation, some things seem, what I call, larger than life at nighttime than they do in the cold light of morning."

Some workers involve the police to increase their personal safety when indications of violence and alcohol abuse are present. As a female MCFD practitioner in a rural community observed:

We travel to some really remote places out here. One intake I had was really late at night and it was alcohol involved and it was out so far, no cell phones worked, the people didn't have running water, they didn't have hydro, and the call was that they were intoxicated ... There was no way on earth I was going to go out there where the bears live ... so the cops came with me and I was very glad they did because when I got there it was fine because the parent was passed out. We couldn't wake them up, but if they wouldn't have been passed out, he was a very large man, who was not pleased at all, about his kids being removed, of course, so it could have been really ugly. And I couldn't have done anything being way out there.

By contrast, a male MCFD practitioner consciously avoided involving the police:

I've been chased out of houses at night, I've ... been threatened, I've had all sorts of things happen, but a lot of those I have to accept responsibility for ... I know that I should be bringing the RCMP. However, the reality ... of child protection is that if I go into a house at night with the RCMP that it's not likely I'm going to get a lot of cooperation, whereas if I am by myself I perhaps get a bit more and it is a little less threatening; however, I am more vulnerable so that's kind of the dilemma that I face, and so you know at times I've made the wrong choice.

Police involvement in child protection is complex. It can increase the practitioner's sense of safety and increase their authority to gain entry to a home, but it can also impede the creation of a trusting relationship with the family.

Building Relationships

One key to personal safety in child protection is a trusting relationship between the practitioner and the family and/or community. The practitioner ceases to be "the stranger at the door" and becomes a person with a name, a face, and a personality. To the social worker the other side of the door is no longer the dangerous unpredictable unknown but, rather, the home of a family with struggles and challenges. An Aboriginal practitioner in an Aboriginal organization described the importance of building relationships and knowing the people: "Most of the people that we need to work with, I've developed a relationship with them, ahead of time, to the point where they trust me, they know who I am, they know why, what kind of job I have. And they open their door and say, 'What can we do?'"

Another Aboriginal social worker in an Aboriginal organization echoed these sentiments:

So they know that we are not just going to come in, give them a few slaps on the wrist or grab their kids or whatever. So then there is dialogue from there. You know, how can we prevent this from happening again? What do you need to do as a parent so it doesn't happen again? How can we effectively help you to ensure that? And so, again, it's much less intrusive, much less conflictual, which reduces the stress load because it is much more stressful to go someplace where you don't know the people and you are starting with no relationship, and you don't really know the issues, so you are just trying to read them as you go.

Aboriginal social workers and MCFD practitioners who have worked in small communities often talk about building trusting relationships with the community. Becoming known in a community and getting to know the community is essential to the personal credibility of the social worker and to effective practice. It is a reciprocal process and is as unique as is the individual and the community, and it reduces uncertainty and stress while creating opportunities for a different kind of practice. But practitioners in regional centres or large metropolitan areas face significant limitations with regard to their ability to know and be known by the community.

Stressful Work

> It's a lot of heavy slogging, a lot of doubt and fear and uncertainty and, stress.
>
> – A non-Aboriginal social worker in
> an Aboriginal organization

MCFD practitioners and non-Aboriginal social workers in Aboriginal organizations describe their work as stressful and speak extensively about it. But Aboriginal practitioners in Aboriginal organizations say little about stress.[2] They refer occasionally to the stressful nature of their clients' lives as well as to the stresses faced by MCFD social workers, but they do not refer to their own stress. One Aboriginal practitioner summed it up this way: "If you ignore the government and just do your community, it isn't stressful at all." However, a social worker employed by the BC MCFD cannot ignore the government. These practitioners identify a number of sources of stress: work volume, paperwork, media interest in child protection, negative office climate, angry clients, absence of trained personnel, lack of management support, isolation, and one's constant visibility in a small community. In some MCFD offices, work volume is a major source of stress. One social worker described her work in an intake office:

> It was just constantly go, go, go. I remember standing there one day, I was on intake, and I had about fifteen to twenty phone messages in my hand. We are standing in the middle of the hallway, didn't know what

---

2   Aboriginal participants indicate that their work is stressful, but they believe that humour, traditional healers, team support, the sense of equality between practitioners and managers, and the freedom to talk about their stressors are factors that minimize stress (Validation of Findings meeting with Aboriginal participants, 14 August 2000). Non-Aboriginal MCFD participants indicated that their stress had quadrupled in the two years since the initial interview (Validation of Findings meeting with MCFD participants, 21 July 2000).

to do, it was 3:00 in the afternoon, I had to return all these messages and I had just dealt with like six or seven intakes, and that was just all phone stuff, that wasn't actually going out to investigate yet. So it was nuts. It was absolutely nuts.

The work volume coupled with the required paperwork creates stress, but the volume impedes the capacity to catch up on paperwork and becomes another source of stress. Teaching oneself to live with unfinished work at the end of a day is essential if one is to reduce stress: "You have to be content with leaving at the end of the day with all sorts of important things undone. You have to be prepared to pray at night that nothing happens to one of your kids in care because you didn't deal with it, because they're going to kill you if it does, and you know there is no way you have of getting to it."

The reality of clients' lives and their pain affects social workers: "The suicides, they're hard and painful. You wonder, could I have done more, should I have done, what could I have done? ... I can remember about three or four times, you know, I've gone home and just cried cause of the pain of it all. But basically, I don't take it home with me too much. You can't or you don't survive." Social workers describe the importance of "not taking all that on personally," but that can be easier to say than to do.

Child protection practice is organized in different ways. Some workers have ongoing responsibility for a caseload and others are focused on short-term intervention at an intake office or after-hours service. In an isolated community, an ongoing caseload is more difficult than is short-term intervention. Two practitioners were able to contrast their work experience in different settings. They clearly preferred short-term practice in an after-hours emergency setting or intake office:

Part of the reason I think that I like nights is it's a one-time involvement and the long-term kind of decision making remains somebody else's responsibility if it's not something that had to be dealt with that day.

It's easier ... there's no question, it's acute, and when you're working you work hard but then you're out of it so you don't carry on an ongoing basis. I don't know too many people that haven't done the intake type of acute crisis work that haven't said that it is easier work. I'm not saying it's easy work, I'm just saying it's easier – it's easier in that you don't deal with the chronic families, day in and day out, and the same situation over and over, and you get the same phone calls day in and day out, so that kind of stuff can wear you down.

Isolation and lack of support often mean a short stay in a small community. One MCFD social worker commented:

Going in I wanted to do three or four years, but just the realization that physically and emotionally I wouldn't be able to go beyond the two years ... I was averaging ten to fifteen hours of overtime every week. Week in and week out. I went thirteen months before my first vacation ... Even when you're gone off camping somewhere the RCMP would come and find you if there was something going on in the community that needed to be dealt with. So it was like you never had your own time where you could shut down and shut it off.

Rapid turnover of staff due to the workload, isolation, and lack of support means that there is often a shortage of trained staff to share the work. Life in a small community also means constant visibility and living with the knowledge that one is practising in a glass bubble.

Child protection is more difficult today because of increased external monitoring. The Office of the Children's Commissioner and the Office of the Child, Youth, and Family Advocate, both of which have conducted inquiries and investigations, are two examples of bodies whose review of practice has added to the stress of social workers. The media's interest in child protection has turned into another form of external monitoring: "Lately we have been in the media a great deal, so that adds a lot in terms of doing your job, constantly being watched, being ... I guess, compared to what's been in the media, whether or not we can do the job." These comments suggest a larger theme common to MCFD practitioners and to some in Aboriginal organizations; that is, the sense of someone looking over your shoulder all the time – of being watched. Some describe it as the need to "jump through a lot of hoops," or the need to "cover your ass," or "cover your bases." These statements suggest a feeling of fear – a fear not of clients but of the system. Some call it paranoia. At its core is the belief that one day your work will be thrust without warning into the spotlight of external review. The media, the children's commissioner, the advocate, the Audit and Review Division, the director of child protection, or all of the above will analyze, question, and critique your decision making in a particular case. One MCFD practitioner described it in the following way: "When you get a case that's really either politically contentious or really high profile all those alarm bells go off in your head because it's like, 'Well that could be me that's being investigated.'" The sense of being watched exacerbates the uncertainty for MCFD practitioners and some in Aboriginal organizations. It leads to the belief that practice conditions are not understood and that the complexity of child protection practice is not recognized.

Complex Work in a Crisis Environment

Assessing a child's risk of harm and deciding whether to remove her is rarely a simple and straightforward procedure. Among the most difficult situations are cases of ongoing neglect where there is a lack of clear evidence. As one practitioner describes it: "Well, there's sometimes families where there's situations like ongoing chronic neglect – the kids are not real clean, we're sure the parents are yelling and screaming, there may be some inappropriate discipline, but you can't prove anything. All you can do is go out and discuss the stuff with them and interview the kids and the kids don't tell you anything and you know there's things going on in the home but you can't do anything about it because there is no evidence of anything."

Sometimes the lack of clarity about how to intervene in a family extends itself to the practitioner in the form of self-doubt: "You kind of wonder, well ... did I actually help these guys or not? Did it help the children? Did it help the parents? Was there any resolve other than us annoying them? You know, people aren't very happy to see us most of the time." Child protection practice is challenging simply due to the complex nature of decision making, but the demands of a large caseload and insufficient time make it even more difficult.

MCFD practitioners as well as some workers in Aboriginal organizations believe that, due to the volume of work, only crisis intervention is possible:

> I deal with emergencies day after day after day. I don't get to close files a lot. I don't get to transfer files. I don't get to do the really nice substantive work that I would like to do, which at times really annoys me a lot.

> It was a lot of basic crisis intervention. It seemed like that's what you had the ability to do, is go in and deal with the crisis, but not to do the long-term work that was needed ... I don't want to call it Band-Aid social work, but I mean that's what was going on. You were running in dealing with the crisis at the moment, dealing with the investigation that needed to be done, or dealing with what the clients perceived as

the crisis for them, and that was kind of the work that you were doing, kind of trying to stay afloat, and making sure that you had covered off what the policy directive was as far as the intake and keeping kids safe. That was our focus.

An Aboriginal practitioner in an Aboriginal organization voiced the same theme: "I do the investigation, and I don't have time to do follow-up, that's very important for me because the families need follow-up. It's not like you get healed and then it's gone. When you have sexual abuse, especially within the family, you need follow-up, ensuring that there is continued healing and continued safety measures and all that stuff." Child protection practice is largely crisis-oriented, and it is difficult to know if intervention has a positive impact. Sometimes the recognition of one's work only comes later.

The in-person contact with clients is one satisfying aspect of child protection work, as is knowing that a difficult, complex, and demanding job has been done well. Some non-Aboriginal practitioners see contact with Aboriginal people, and the opportunity to learn from them, as a satisfying aspect of child protection practice. However, the lack of positive recognition from the public, the families served, the media, and/or management is difficult. It seems that workers must meet the challenge of being able to function daily with few positives. Sometimes clients provide feedback to a practitioner's intervention at a later time, and several practitioners provided examples of clients who wrote or returned at a later date to let them know their intervention had been beneficial:

I knew all along that I did the right thing, but for a parent to come back and say, "Thank-you for doing that because I couldn't care for my child." Yeah, so you know there are those moments that happen but they're few and far between. You know, a kid writes you a thank-you card or gives you a big hug and you can see that you've had a real positive impact on a kid's life, and that doesn't happen very often either.

Sometimes, when a family calls up and again asks for help, practitioners realize that an earlier intervention has been helpful:

I remember apprehending these, these children, two girls in ___, and they were very difficult and I would take them to a resource and they would go in the front door and go out the back door and they got

involved with prostitution ... it must have been just after I moved to
____, I got a letter from one of these girls and she was married and had
children, and was thankful for my intervention and, you know, they
seemed to grow up, and because at the time you think, "Oh, you are
doing nothing except hitting your head against the wall ..." I try to tell
my colleagues who are fairly new in the field, because they get discouraged, that ... change happens later. Like they may see it years down the
road.

5
The Sociopolitical Practice Context

The Ministry is moving to a place that is about policy-driven
child welfare practice and that scares me.

– An Aboriginal social worker

The 1990s in British Columbia was a time of extensive and rapid change
to the legislation and organization of child protection practice. Not only
was new legislation introduced (1994) and proclaimed (1996), but a
major reorganization of services occurred (1996-97), and the first judicial inquiry into a child protection case was completed (1994-95). At
the same time new offices were created whose functions included the
review of child protection practice. These were the Office of the Child,
Youth, and Family Advocate (1994-2001) and the Office of the Children's Commissioner (1997). During this period there was extensive
ongoing media interest in issues of child protection. The hearings of
the Gove Inquiry (1994-95), the revelation of additional children's deaths
in the summer of 1996, and the removal of seventy-one children from
their families in Quesnel, British Columbia, in February 1998 were periods of intense media interest.

From 1980 to the present Aboriginal child welfare has undergone extensive changes. The first Aboriginal child welfare organization began
with the Spallumcheen Band in 1980 and was followed by the second
with the Nuu-Chah-Nulth Tribal Council (Vancouver Island) in 1985.
In March 1996 the province created an Aboriginal Relations Branch and
Policy Division within the Social Services Ministry to respond to interest in the creation of Aboriginal child welfare organizations. By 2004
there were twenty approved agreements for the provision of child protection services that cover approximately 50 percent of the 200 bands
in British Columbia. These twenty agreements also include a Métis

organization in the South Fraser region of Greater Vancouver and an urban child welfare organization in Vancouver/Richmond. An additional forty bands are now planning the development of an Aboriginal child welfare organization (BC Ministry of Children and Family Development 2004). This chapter explores the impact of these legislative and organizational changes as well as the impact of the Gove Inquiry and media interest on how social workers think about practice.

Legislation and Policy

Practitioners describe the significance of the Child, Family, and Community Service Act (1994) in a variety of ways. Some view it positively and cite the emphasis on enshrining children's rights in legislation, the use of less intrusive measures, and the addition of the "likely-to-be-abused" clause. Others view the act as well intentioned but are concerned about its complex and expansive policy requirements as well as about the lack of resources to implement its aims. Some see themselves caught between the aims of the legislation and their ability to deliver. As one MCFD practitioner commented: "I think what people are saying is that it's too much ... It's not the policy per se, it's not the requirements, it's not the comprehensive risk assessment or the comprehensive plans of care or the rights of children in care or any of that stuff that they object to, it's their ability to do it in the framework of the workload."

Faced with a gap between good legislative aims, expansive policy requirements, and an inability to deliver, practitioners respond in different ways. Some become "policy-driven"; that is, they respond to the complexity of policy and legislation by trying to fulfill all requirements but, in doing so, lose sight of the human beings being served. One MCFD supervisor described the pressures that policy-driven practice put on practitioners: "We have an enormous tightening of rules, regulations and expectations around how child protection is done. It's as if administration, government, has tried to be prescriptive about child protection to the nth degree – as if every possible variable in a child protection situation can be quantified on a computer system or in a paperwork accountability system." An Aboriginal supervisor from an Aboriginal organization concurred: "The ministry is moving to a place that is about policy-driven child welfare practice and that scares me ... I think that policy moves workers and their clients to not very equal places as far as power [is concerned] and I don't think that it lends a whole lot of room for change." Faced with the demand to follow policy, some practitioners end up practising with less discretion, humanity, and flexibility, and they sometimes see policy where it doesn't exist.

The second response practitioners make to the gap between the demands of legislation/policy and their ability to respond is to ignore policy. One MCFD practitioner commented: "I do look at my policy books, but for the most part I just kind of go along with [how] I think ... it should go. So, in principle, I think I follow what my mandate is and what I'm supposed to do. I don't follow, like, exactly cross my T's and dot my I's, according to policy because ... it's not very user-friendly." The third response is to "stretch" policy to fit the needs of a particular child, family, or community. In the words of one MCFD practitioner: "I think that the smaller the community, the more isolated, the fewer workers you have, the more innovative that you need to become, and so I think what you do is you tend to stretch policy and maybe even legislative stuff a bit more than you would in areas that are better serviced."

Some MCFD practitioners expressed ambivalence about the impact of the new legislation. One saw it as part of moving towards more intrusion in family life, while another saw it as providing the potential for more removals through the new "likely-to-be-abused" clause. Two MCFD practitioners found it difficult to fully assess the impact of the new legislation because several sections (youth agreements, family conferences) had yet to be implemented. Another MCFD practitioner believed that the legislation did not recognize the extended family or community in its planning and thus failed to ensure children's safety.

By contrast, Aboriginal practitioners in Aboriginal organizations generally saw the legislation as having little impact on their practice. One commented: "It didn't really hit us in any way. It's sort of like things we already practised." Another saw the new legislation as a First Nations model in which the whole community was involved: "That whole concept or idea has been a part of First Nations values and culture and history for a long time ... The new legislation doesn't directly impact our band and the way our business is conducted, other than [that] we might have adapted some of their forms or liked some of their ideas and utilized them." This Aboriginal practitioner argued that the significance of the new act is minimal because it merely "catches up" with existing First Nations ideas and practices, incorporating them into legislation. To another, the legislation and policy is a fairly minor aspect of her work. To her, the authority to practice child protection is derived from the community, not from provincial legislation:

We get our authority from the bands in order to do our job, and that is where we get our authority, although we get the rights from the ministry, you know, under their guidelines. They have got these two binders of policies and procedures. They are this thick. I have barely opened them, just because ... the way we deliver our services is a bit different ... I think unconsciously we may follow a lot of the guidelines that they do use, but we barely refer to their manuals ... unless we need something that we have never done.

Part of the reason why legislation and policy is in the background is because it is viewed as being external to the community: "The laws we work within are theirs not ours, not our peoples'." This practitioner expressed the concern that many Aboriginal practitioners have about the legislation and its power: it symbolizes the imposition of the dominant society's cultural standards and practices – standards and practices that are foreign to Aboriginal communities. To another Aboriginal practitioner this situation created a special demand on Aboriginal practitioners, organizations, and communities to critique policy in order to determine its cultural fit with their community. One practitioner believed that the concept of delegated authority needs to be critiqued:

I mean, when I look at delegation, I mean there's a whole myth on this conception around delegation. Delegation is simply that. It's delegation of responsibilities and duties by the director. There is no such thing as a transfer. I mean, it is not given to us because the director still has a role and the Ministry for Children and Families has a vested interest in maintaining an Aboriginal caseload ... We've now shifted to looking at delegated confirmation agreements, but basically the agreements with the director still say that the director maintains responsibility and ownership for programs that happen on-reserve. Ultimately, the director is accountable.

This Aboriginal practitioner also critiqued the new legislation: "The legislation promised ... that it would impact the work of social workers drastically, that it would reduce the paperwork, it would reduce the amount of court work, it would ensure more community involvement, it would ensure that the subsequent restructuring at the ministry would support Aboriginal needs. None of that has come [in]to play."

External Review of Practice
In 1994, at the same time as the Child, Family, and Community Services Act was passed, legislation created the Office of the Child, Youth, and Family Advocate in order to provide an advocacy mechanism for children, youth, and families in relation to public services but at arm's-

length from the public service. Three years later, in 1997, the Office of the Children's Commissioner was created to investigate child fatalities and critical injuries that occurred to children in care as well as to review plans for care. In a short period of time practitioners were confronted with two new mechanisms for the external review of practice. These new mechanisms were in addition to the Ombudsman's Office, the director of child protection, and the Audit and Review Division of the MCFD. Views about the impact of these offices on practice ranged from very positive to very negative. Some spoke enthusiastically about the Office of the Advocate and saw it as "another avenue for recourse ... [because] the state makes a very poor parent." They felt that it recognized that "children need to have a voice." One Aboriginal practitioner felt that it would make social workers be "a little bit more on their toes" because it was one more body "looking over the shoulders" of social workers. However, this perspective was not supported by others. To some in Aboriginal organizations the Office of the Child, Youth, and Family Advocate was irrelevant to community-based approaches to advocacy: "I don't think people here would so much use her as they would just go to their chiefs or to the Tribal Council if they aren't happy rather than go to another ... [outside body] like her."

Another Aboriginal practitioner suggested that her community would use childcare workers, community elders, or traditional people for advocacy. Only one MCFD practitioner expressed opposition to the concept: "We need to have a genuine commitment to adequate staffing levels for the expectations that are laid upon us by management ... We don't need any more advocates, we need people out here who can do the work." The Office of the Children's Commissioner met with a mixed response from practitioners as well. Some felt it had little or no impact on their practice, while others felt that its impact was profound. One non-Aboriginal practitioner in an Aboriginal organization commented:

> This children's commissioner that they developed – there is such a conflict between the act and the children's commissioner that you're almost working in a schizophrenic environment ... The children's commissioner has created a paranoia cover-your-butt attitude or you're gonna get slapped ... Cases where I've been involved with the children's commissioner, that's usually when something has happened and there's a crisis on your caseload because they're not involved with minor stuff. So you're trying to deal with this crisis on your caseload and you're having to send these reports down to Victoria in a short period of time and they're going to Victoria so you want to make sure that

they're done properly, and they're accurate, and there's everything in there, and so then you get them starting to call you and questioning, you know, your every action ... and I think it just creates a paranoid environment ... Rather than having any useful suggestions that maybe you can do this, they're just creating this paper overload, and I don't think any of them have been even out in the field.

This practitioner also commented that, although the organization was criticized by the children's commissioner for the way it handled a youth suicide the year before, no new resources had been created in the interval and another youth was now at risk of suicide.

Two practitioners, both of whom are supervisors, described the potentially damaging impact of the children's commissioner's investigations on staff, and they stressed the importance of the office "reframing" its interventions. One MCFD supervisor described his approach as follows: "What I try and say to them is, how many social workers have you even heard of that have ever been fired or even disciplined as a result of it? ... Not very many and the ones that you have [heard of] have usually been justifiable to some degree, so you try and battle against that." An Aboriginal supervisor in an Aboriginal organization commented: "I think it makes me more creative in reframing that stuff for workers in that it is not about, you know, [a] personal attack on your practice but that we can use this for learning and looking as well. How could we have done this different?" Some Aboriginal practitioners in Aboriginal organizations had no awareness of the office and no understanding of its functions. There is a sense that this office, much like the Office of the Child, Youth, and Family Advocate, is a distant, unknown entity essentially irrelevant to everyday practice.

Gove Inquiry into Child Protection
Judge Gove's inquiry into the death of Matthew Vaudreuil was a pivotal point in the history of child protection practice in British Columbia. It took place from the summer of 1994 to November 1995 and was surrounded by extensive media coverage. Gove's three-volume report was widely circulated, broadly discussed, and led to significant changes in the new Child, Family, and Community Services Act.[3] At the inquiry's public hearings, the actions of social workers involved in the case were carefully examined and reported in the media. The impact of the Gove

---

3   During the inquiry process, Judge Gove sought and obtained amendments to the new act through an interim report to the government.

Inquiry within the Ministry of Children and Family Development was profound. Some MCFD practitioners who were friends of those testifying "couldn't believe the change in them ... after being put through the stand." Others described it as being "basically like an inquisition." Some were "frightened of the implications for them personally from systemic problems," whereas others looked at it and saw it as operating according to the theory of "guilty until proven innocent, that means scapegoating." Others recognized that "any one of us could have been possibly in that same predicament because a lot of times you can get files and all that. You do your best [to] try to read through it. You get a grasp. You hope you are doing the right thing, but, in all honesty, any point in time a child can die in your caseload, and you hope that you have the support ... of your ministry or your employer, but that just showed us that you don't, that basically it's you."

Some believed it led to a "cover-your-ass" attitude, as this practitioner illustrates:

> Prior to Gove there would be a situation, say it's like an intake, you know, mom or dad gets a little bit excessive with the physical discipline, maybe using an instrument, like say a wooden spoon or a stick, something that wasn't unheard of, say twenty-five to thirty years ago. That was pretty much parental practice ... Prior to Gove you would say, "OK, look, we've talked to you about discipline, this can't occur, and you need to take this parenting course. We'll get a childcare worker, whatever, somebody to help monitor – what other kind of supports do you think you need?" So it would be more of a supportive, you know, you can't do that kind of thing, but after Gove, if you had a second, third possibly report of the same kind of thing – kids out of the home. You do this, this, and this and then you can get your kids back ... so it went more intrusively into the family.

Some believe it led to a zero tolerance for children's deaths, where there was an expectation "that we actually will save every child in this province." One of the consequences of intake workers' "erring on the side of caution" was increased removals. Another practitioner described it as "when in doubt, take them out."

Through the inquiry process, some believed, the "public really lost a lot of respect for social workers." Overall, a feeling of panic gripped the system, and this influenced child protection decision making, as may be seen in the following comment from an MCFD practitioner:

I had a really simple intake one day. I thought it was quite simple. I don't even remember now what it was, but I just remember I handled it ... I-don't-want-anything-to-happen-on-my-shift kind of thing, and I took care of this intake to a place where I was comfortable with it, and usually I do more than most people would tell me to do. Anyway, my DS wasn't here, phoned another DS in the region to get some feedback, and it was just bizarre the reaction. I actually had to make this person slow down and [said], "Whoa, whoa, hold on a minute, this is what I am saying. This is what the report was, this is what happened. This is what is going to happen. Why would you think I have to remove these kids?" ... People are much more on edge, and they are much quicker to remove kids than they would have been in the past.

Some practitioners argue that the changes in practice direction predate the Gove Inquiry, whereas others believe the changes were due to the interaction between senior management, the Gove Inquiry, and the new legislation. However, most practitioners seem to agree that the Gove Inquiry was a pivotal point. It "reinforced the message around accountable service delivery," "became a benchmark ... to staff where some of the shortcomings are," had "a lot of really good suggestions," and tried "to standardize social work practice around the province." However, more significantly, the Gove Inquiry communicated to practitioners that their practice was "under scrutiny all the time" and that they could be sought out and placed under a spotlight at any moment. As a consequence, MCFD practitioners reported that they now "double-check on things" more often, consult more extensively with their supervisor, take fewer risks, act more intrusively, and remove children more readily than they did before.

The Gove Inquiry had a different and subtler impact on Aboriginal practitioners in Aboriginal organizations than it did on MCFD practitioners. It essentially suggested two guidelines for practice: "be thorough" and "take action." To one practitioner, being thorough meant: "we just don't overlook anything, if there is a concern, then we totally investigate it, thoroughly, in a way where it is respectable and we realistically look at it, with the families, with the social worker that works on-reserve with us, the community." To another Aboriginal practitioner taking action meant: "Oh, this could be like a Gove. You know, meaning the death of a child ... I think when they say, 'This could be a Gove' [it] is an expression of stress, like we have to address this ... We have to get in there and do something." Although thorough investigation may lead to closer monitoring, there is no suggestion that it leads to more removals: "We can't be there every minute to watch ... so we have extended family and community working with us, on-reserve, so that really helps us keep an eye on it ... So, yes, the Gove Inquiry really helped us to become more aware of staying on top of all of these cases."

Media Interest in Child Protection

Today's child protection practitioner lives with the ongoing possibility that her practice will come under media scrutiny.[4] Whether it is a child's death, a judicial decision, legal action by a former child-in-care, public anger at excessive government action or inaction, a complaint from the members of a family or community whose child has been removed, or an investigative body publishing a report, child protection practice generates news. Stories of children's vulnerability juxtaposed with the exercise of parental authority or state power, sometimes against a backdrop of violence or sex, create ongoing public demand for information. Such an environment generates a range of practitioner responses. Some welcome media interest in their work and view it positively. Others see it as negative, inaccurate, and misleading. One Aboriginal practitioner in an Aboriginal organization viewed the media's interest in child protection as a good thing:

> Child welfare has been a monopoly nationally that has not undergone a whole lot of scrutiny and I think that ... the ministry has a responsibility to the community to make the community aware of what's happening ... The media can sensationalize things, but the media can also bring to the forefront what the issues are ... I think the media representation of child welfare is a good thing, and I hope that continues. I hope that child welfare continues to be number one on the political agenda and media agenda because it hasn't been historically.

One MCFD practitioner believed that child protection was complex, but that this complexity was not reflected in media reports: "I think knowing about the subject takes a lot of knowledge and a fair amount of research and I don't think people are willing to put in the time. [They're] willing to take information on face value and go with it, particularly if it's something that is going to play on people's emotions, and so I don't think that people take the time to present the information in a balanced informative way." A consistent theme in practitioners'

---

4   When referring to practitioners I use the feminine pronoun to avoid awkward sentence constructions.

reflections about the media is the tendency to report negative rather than positive news about child protection: "Whenever there is a case that comes to the papers, and if they see it as a social worker's neglect, that makes news. But they never hear about all the good things that's happened with families out there."

To some MCFD practitioners the negative imagery of child protection practice leads to a politicized work environment characterized by reactive practice. It also intensifies difficult working conditions for practitioners and creates strained relationships with clients, community professionals, and Aboriginal communities. As one MCFD practitioner commented: "Sometimes it affects us in terms of establishing a credibility with other professionals in the community who maybe tend to read the negative information about social workers and then tar us all with the same brush." Within Aboriginal communities, the media portrayal of child protection removals recreates earlier images of practice. One MCFD practitioner described a recent conversation with members of an Aboriginal community about child protection practitioners: "You're just going to come out and take our children. There was rumours that up in Quesnel ... that a bus showed up during the night with the social workers and they came out and took, snatched children in the dark." This practitioner described the image of child protection practice recreated by the media as "the stork taking children and giving them to somebody else."

Although media scrutiny of practice leads some practitioners to become more cautious, to double-check their work, and to make sure their actions are well documented, it leads others to recognize that child protection practice is political. Some welcome the media's interest in child protection as a sign that children's issues are gaining increasing importance on the political agenda, but others are angry because media representations of child protection practice have negative effects on clients, professionals, and communities. A case in point is the media coverage given to the removal of seventy-one children in Quesnel, British Columbia in February 1998.[5]

According to MCFD management, the removals were necessary as the children had been left "at risk" by district social workers. A special team was assembled from across British Columbia to conduct the investigations and removals. Many of the children were Aboriginal, and their

---

5   Quesnel is a town of 11,000, about 660 kilometres north of Vancouver. The removals occurred four to sixteen months prior to the interviews for this book.

removal attracted national media attention and responses from the Assembly of First Nations and Status of Women Canada. Practitioners had a range of responses to these events. To two Aboriginal practitioners, it recreated an older representation of child protection practice with the Aboriginal community – the sixties scoop. One Aboriginal practitioner employed in an Aboriginal organization described it as follows:

> What a shocker. It was very shocking to me ... That's the first impression I got when I heard about that, was these massive amount of families that had children removed from them and ... it reminded me of the sixties scoop, where kids on-reserve were taken without even the parents being aware of them [being] taken. It brings up a lot of memories ... I don't know if you have seen these different videos where they have shown how airplanes would go into places and just haul the kids on the airplane without parents being aware and taking off with them.

Another Aboriginal practitioner employed by the MCFD saw it this way: "it sure made a dirty name for the ministry social workers and it brings up those old issues of 'just want to take kids away and don't even ask questions' or 'they don't even do their job,' and just all the bad negative stuff that social workers do ... that really brought up that old feeling ... you're just coming in to scoop kids and you don't even care, you don't understand, and it really brought up a lot of stuff like that."

To some MCFD practitioners the removals were testimony to the excessive workload faced by child protection workers. However, as one practitioner noted, part of the workload issue is inadequate staff and inexperienced workers: "Quesnel is one of the areas where traditionally they've had a hard time with staffing as well as a lot of other areas further north ... So, there's a lot of issues when you have staffing that's (a) new, (b) there's not enough of them ... there's pretty high turnover rates." To some Aboriginal practitioners, the child protection practice in Quesnel expressed a difference in approach:

> They used a lot of VCA's or what I call Voluntary Care Agreements. You know, that is what we do here as well. We would rather work with the parents because I understand the workers there had a relationship with the parents and were providing services to support the parents while the children were in their homes rather than removing them. And so that is what we would do. We would work with the parents if the parents said, "Well, I am in a place now where I really can't take care of my kids," you know, we would work with that because that is where the

parent is at ... And you have got to work that way in a small community. I mean, if we were to go to court with the number of cases that each one of us is managing ... a case a week or something like that ... our staff would be busy in paperwork. They wouldn't be able to be out there meeting families in the communities, doing home visits, and connecting with children.

The Quesnel incident generated a range of interpretations and explanations among practitioners and suggested several "guides for action" to practitioners. To some, it recreated images of child protection practice found in British Columbia during the 1960s within the Aboriginal community. As such, it reintroduced issues of credibility and trust between practitioners employed by the BC MCFD and members of the Aboriginal community. To others, it confirmed the ministry's lack of support for a family-oriented approach to practice and reasserted the importance of child removals. In this sense it was a message to practitioners to double-check their work and to be cautious about leaving a child in the care of the family. Although some practitioners saw this incident as an expression of the stress and workload facing MCFD practitioners (clearly identifying with the potential for this incident to occur in their offices), others believed the incident to be foreign to their practice reality and saw it as having no impact on them, their practice, or their community.

Politics and Child Protection Practice

Child protection practice, as it pertains to Aboriginal children in British Columbia, takes place within a complex, rapidly changing context. The MCFD practitioner is accountable to the hierarchy of officials within the ministry, beginning with the team leader and extending upward to the minister. At the same time, she is accountable to review bodies such as the Audit and Review Division of MCFD; the Office of the Children's Commissioner; the Office of the Child, Youth, and Family Advocate; and the Office of the Ombudsman. The legacy of the Gove Inquiry, with its public questioning of social workers and its extensive media coverage, has generated a fear that the action of any practitioner could, at some unpredictable moment, be thrown into the spotlight of managerial, media, and external review. Highly publicized child protection controversies subsequent to the Gove Inquiry, such as the Quesnel incident, confirm for MCFD practitioners that they could be blamed as individuals or "found guilty until proven innocent." At times there are paranoiac overtones to how MCFD practitioners express these pressures.

Aboriginal practitioners represent the pressures described above in much more muted tones than do MCFD practitioners. The new Child, Family, and Community Services Act and its complex policy manuals are conveyed either as (1) the representation of a First Nations model of child welfare that has finally received recognition or as (2) essentially irrelevant to the day-to-day practice of child protection. External review bodies, such as the Office of the Children's Commissioner and the Office of the Child, Youth, and Family Advocate, are often seen as distant shadows that have little direct impact on practice. Knowledge about their functions is minimal, and consciousness about their significance to practice is vague and ill-defined. Although these bodies have the potential to scrutinize the practice of most Aboriginal practitioners, the elements of fear, paranoia, and apprehension found among MCFD practitioners are largely absent from Aboriginal practitioners (particularly those outside the MCFD).

However, Aboriginal practitioners, particularly those in Aboriginal organizations, identify different pressures than those named by MCFD practitioners. To them, the most significant pressure involves the constraint against cultural autonomy, the lack of freedom to protect children in ways consistent with the values, traditions, and practices of their community. Their fear is that the policies, practices, and systems of the dominant society, expressed by the government and laws of British Columbia and Canada, will control child welfare in ways inconsistent with community practices. For example, the legal sanction to intervene in family life derives from the provincial Child Family and Community Services Act, the procedures are taken from the policy manuals of the BC MCFD, and the funding is provided by both the Government of Canada and the Government of British Columbia. This matrix of law, policy, and resources creates pressure towards uniformity, towards adapting to the norms of the dominant society. To Aboriginal practitioners this ignores differences in history, culture, and identity that are integral to child protection practice as it pertains to Aboriginal children. One Aboriginal practitioner sums up this pressure as "continually doing the battle of not creating the ministry on reserve."

However, there is also a complex interplay of regulatory systems and resources that creates an additional pressure, which is described by Aboriginal practitioners in Aboriginal organizations. Although funding is derived from the federal and provincial governments, the responsibility for funding preventive and early intervention services in Aboriginal communities is unclear. The inability to fund such "less disruptive measures," which is called for by the provincial legislation, affects the community's ability to support a family in ways consistent both with the legislation and with community values and practices. Placement in alternate care, which is funded by the federal government, becomes the only means to support the family (simply because it is available). Preventive services, such as those provided by a childcare worker, home-maker, respite care worker, as well as cultural activities are not funded. An Aboriginal practitioner described this issue in the following way: "We don't have an equitable playing field on-reserve, and what we know is that [our] people, for the most part, are reluctant to use off-reserve services, and so what we know is that we need to build our own pro-grams ... what you know from experience is that if I had six prevention social workers that I'd only need two child safety workers."

In addition to the funding of prevention services in Aboriginal com-munities, another pressure confronting Aboriginal organizations is the BC MCFD's "off-loading" of Aboriginal youth onto an Aboriginal child welfare organization. Previously these youth were in the care of MCFD, but they are now being returned to Aboriginal communities. This proc-ess, described by one Aboriginal practitioner as "plopping," is the in-verse of the sixties scoop. The trend can be viewed positively as recognizing the responsibility of the Aboriginal community to care for its children. At the same time, when children have particular needs but the Aboriginal community does not have the services to meet them, then this trend creates a condition of "responsibility without resources." It adds pressure to the practitioner and the community, particularly when little is known about the youth and there is little connection to the community. The absence of support services results in inequity. The services available to an Aboriginal child in her/his own community are fewer than those available to an Aboriginal child in the care of MCFD. An Aboriginal practitioner described the situation in one community:

The ministry doesn't want to deal with them anymore. And so if they ... know there's an Aboriginal connection, they just want to wipe their hands of it and we don't have the history on those kids, we don't know why they were put into care to start with, or where they have been, or what kind of family they were in or what their life, for the past fourteen years, has been like ... Like we didn't really deal with any until probably the last couple of years, but this past year, there has probably been at least six. At least six really hard kids, you know, that are in trouble with the law and ... just not succeeding at all. They don't know the community, they don't know any members up there, they know they are connected, but they don't know anything about their families.

Aboriginal practitioners in Aboriginal organizations recognize that there is a political dimension to child protection practice, but they tend to see it as originating in the imposition of foreign laws, policies, and systems. In relation to the politics of the local community, one practitioner noted that there are clear guidelines to separate child protection practice from political intervention on the part of community members: "Anything political that enters into my job, our admin director here has totally stated that we are not to deal with anything political. That is to be directed to him. So the director and the board deals with it."

Aboriginal practitioners are aware of pressures on their practice, but cultural autonomy and the adequacy of funding headlines their list of preoccupations. Sometimes they demonstrate an awareness of the pressures that affect the practice of their MCFD colleagues as, for example, when they share their concerns about the external scrutiny of practice. However, unlike MCFD practitioners, Aboriginal practitioners do not depict the Gove Inquiry; the Office of the Children's Commissioner; the Office of the Child, Youth, and Family Advocate; the media; and the new legislation and policy as prominent in their list of pressures.

Although "post-inquiry paranoia" is not visible in the discourse of Aboriginal practitioners, they do have a fear that is unique to them – the "fear of encroachment." They fear that the values, policies, and practices of the MCFD will creep up on Aboriginal communities and inhibit the ability of Aboriginal people to protect children in their own ways. This common fear suggests that there is a "code of social exchange" among Aboriginal practitioners concerning what constitutes good child protection practice.

To the MCFD practitioner multiple pressures create a dynamic interplay between context, ideas, and actions. One result of this is an orientation towards child protection practice that is cautious, low-risk, thorough, fully documented, and rule-oriented. Some describe this as "policy-driven" practice, and its principal indicator is a tendency to remove children from the family sooner rather than later. It is suggestive of the need practitioners have to create a level of professional certainty for themselves within a climate of intense uncertainty. Its consequence is the removal of creativity from thinking and action about practice because creativity constitutes "risk" – to oneself, to one's clients, to one's family, and to one's future at MCFD. Although one MCFD practitioner said, "I don't do politics," most would tend towards the view of another, who said, "I believe politics is involved in just about everything."

Whether it is the decision to remove a child, to protest a protection decision, to review a file, to write a news story, to appoint a public inquiry, to discipline a practitioner, or to overturn a decision, child protection practice is understood to be a form of political activity.

For some, the knowledge that child protection practice is replete with political decision making is accompanied by disillusion. It is as though words and actions don't match, as though one's professional life as a child protection practitioner is lived within contradictory realities. Child protection practice is about keeping children safe, but it is also about keeping the minister for children and family development and senior officials safe from political embarrassment. It is about using "least intrusive measures" to ensure a child's safety; however, when such measures do not exist, or when they constitute a creative interventive risk, it is about using the most intrusive measure possible – a removal – because it avoids potential negative sanctions within a climate of cautious, low-risk practice. To MCFD practitioners, following policy, avoiding risk, and recognizing child protection practice as political constitutes the "common sense" everyday knowledge they have of their working world.

6
Organizational Context of Practice

There's no map, I mean there is a map that doesn't belong to us, but there is no map in how do you create an Aboriginal child welfare agency?

          – An Aboriginal social worker

Culturally distinct organizational contexts for child welfare practice developed in Canada after 1980 as Aboriginal child welfare organizations emerged distinct from "mainstream" organizations (RCAP 1996, 3, 30). In British Columbia, these contexts are, principally, band or tribal child welfare organizations and the BC Ministry of Children and Family Development.[6] This chapter begins with a description of organizational life at the ministry and then considers life in Aboriginal child welfare organizations in British Columbia. It describes both from the practitioner's point of view.

The BC MCFD is a large provincial government ministry with approximately 4,500 employees. Aboriginal child welfare organizations have approximately six to forty employees each, are under the general auspices of a band or tribal council, often operate through tripartite agreements with the Province of British Columbia and the Government of Canada, and are managed by a community-based board of directors.

Beginning in 1980 changes to the organization of Aboriginal child welfare services began. The Spallumcheen Band became the first band in the province to provide child welfare services directly to its members. Its child welfare service operates under the authority of a band bylaw and is outside provincial jurisdiction. Between 1985 and 1999

---

6 For a fuller discussion of this point, see Chapter 3.

an additional sixteen Aboriginal child welfare organizations began operation, with the delegated authority of the provincial director of child protection. Now there are twenty approved agreements for the provision of child protection services, and they cover approximately 50 percent of the 200 bands in British Columbia. These agreements include a Métis organization in the South Fraser region of Greater Vancouver and an urban child welfare organization in Vancouver/Richmond. An additional forty bands are planning the development of an Aboriginal child welfare organization at this time (BC Ministry for Children and Family Development 2004).

As discussed in previous chapters, there were extensive changes to the legislation, policy, and organizational context of child welfare services in British Columbia during the 1990s. These include the proclamation of the Child, Family, and Community Services Act, 1996; the first judicial inquiry into a child protection case, known as the Gove Inquiry (1994-95); two new external review mechanisms (the Office of the Child, Youth, and Family Advocate created in 1995 [abolished in 2001] and the Office of the Children's Commissioner created in 1997; new policy, procedure, and computer protocols; and the reorganization of provincial services to children and families in 1997 with the creation of the BC Ministry for Children and Families (later renamed the Ministry of Children and Family Development).

Ministry of Children and Family Development
Practitioners' experience of organizational life at the BC Ministry of Children and Family Development is summed up in four phrases: "out there on a limb," "under a microscope," "walking on eggshells," and "my goose is cooked." The first phrase describes the lack of organizational safety practitioners' experience in their work. Practice demands independent judgment, or "thinking on your feet," but many felt that their creative interventions had no assurance of management support. "Under a microscope" spoke to the ways in which everyday practice is subject to careful examination by others. "Walking on eggshells" implies that the foundation of support for one's practice is very delicate and could collapse at any moment. "My goose is cooked" describes the point at which a review of a practitioner's work is undertaken, errors found, and a process of discipline enacted that could lead to suspension or termination. Taken together these phrases provide a thumbnail sketch of practitioners' reality at MCFD. They depict the practitioner's living and working within a climate of organizational uncertainty. On the one hand, there are management expectations that the worker will fulfill the require-

ments of child protection legislation and policy; on the other hand, there is knowledge that if her intervention enters the spotlight of media scrutiny or external review it could unleash a search whose purpose is to fix blame. These beliefs influence social workers to move towards a practice orientation that is cautious, low-risk, and highly compliant with policy.

Extensive changes to policy, organization, structure, and the delivery of child protection services in British Columbia took place immediately prior to the interviews conducted for *Protecting Aboriginal Children*. Some MCFD practitioners acknowledge the positive aspects of these changes but, overall, see them as being too many, too fast. The cumulative effect of this has meant less time for clients and more energy focused on system requirements. As one MCFD social worker observed, "A trend over the last five years is for an ever-increasing amount of office work accountability in the practice of child protection ... It lacks the space for worker judgment. It lacks a recognition of the richness of human beings."

Accompanying the massive changes is a sense of disillusion. One MCFD social worker described it as "weariness with change," with confusion being one of the by-products. A practitioner in an Aboriginal organization stated: "It has made it more difficult to contact people. For example, the mental health worker here ... used to be really accessible. You'd ring him on the phone and he'd actually come on the phone when you called him and now you call the Ministry for Children and Families to get hold of him and you get that he is not at his desk and that he will return your call and, you know, you can play phone tag forever with him."[7]

The impact of the many changes involves both a sense of disillusion with regard to change and a "loss of vision" with regard to practice. One MCFD practitioner described colleagues accepting "the ministry's reality" and making decisions "within this reality." To this social worker, the ministry's reality involves "not questioning the ability to question." Overall, practitioners expressed disillusion not only with organizational changes but also with the ability to question, to talk about practice, and to disagree with the ministry's direction. The inability to question, talk, and disagree reinforces practice oriented towards standardization and control – a practice permeated with fear of the disciplinary consequences of deviation.

---

7   Ministry for Children and Families was the ministry's name at the time of the interviews.

Child protection practice functions within power relationships. Management has the power to discipline workers, the children's commissioner has the power to review cases, and the Legislature has the power to amend legislation and to establish the level of resources available for practice. But the most fundamental power relationship is the practitioner's power to remove a child from her/his parents. At MCFD power relationships are expressed through passive resistance, aggression, and the use of the "power button." One MCFD social worker described a lot of "passive resistance stuff" in relation to organizational change, especially the "incredible resistance ... about having to become a part of a ministry that is so bureaucratized and so accountable in so many places." Another described a tendency to become "more aggressive" in practice: "I tend to stand up for things a little bit more, I think. And it comes from being involved in an aggressive system. You learn to survive ... If you walk into a volatile situation all meek and timid, you're going to get crushed real quick." A third described using the power button to reinforce the existing power imbalance: "it's like knowing that you have that power, that you can take a child from the family or you have that authority ... that you can split up a family ... for some people ... they think that's [the] be all and end all ... You can tell by their tone they use it on the people and all that, it's like their thing, they can do it. Like if you don't do what I say I'm going to pull your child."

These expressions of power at the ministry could be an extension of management's exercise of power over practitioners. Several MCFD social workers were clear about the sense of fear and paranoia that pervades the MCFD atmosphere. Practitioners can take this atmosphere with them when they enter the home of a family. For example, if a social worker blames parents for the quality of child care, this will increase the family's fear and paranoia. This may be an extension of management's tendency to blame an individual social worker when a child is injured or dies. MCFD social workers believe there is a noticeable tendency to blame without sharing responsibility: "It's the line worker where the buck stops, they're the ones that, you know, get all the publicity, and the ministry or the politicians don't take any ownership ... But I think the people in Victoria and politicians have to take ownership as well, like it's just not one person, it's the system." At its core, power expresses itself in the power to blame, the power to share responsibility, and the power to empower or disempower. The imbalance of power in the system conditions the relationships within it. As one MCFD practitioner noted: "There is always somebody who has power over somebody else in the system."

All MCFD social workers described workload as having a major impact on the quality of their practice. The factors most often cited to explain the excessive workload are the amount of paperwork, the size of the caseload, and the frequent turnover of staff. MCFD practitioners describe the caseload as ranging from forty to ninety-two. But caseload size does not provide an indication of the complexity of work or the amount of travel involved. When a practitioner in a rural community is required to travel seven or eight hours to meet a family, a one-hour visit to assess a child's safety can take two days. Similarly, caseload size gives no indication of the complexity of the work involved when dealing with a family. Five complex cases can be an excessive workload, depending on the nature of the work. One MCFD practitioner expressed what others said in other ways: "The workload is just outrageous." The excessive workload is an ongoing source of stress to MCFD practitioners, and it leads to forms of practice aimed at "just keeping your head above water." Managing a caseload of forty to ninety-two also means superficial intervention and reactive practice. This leads to a lack of cultural understanding about Aboriginal children and families and results in a bias towards using MCFD resources rather than placing children with the extended family. A supervisor in an Aboriginal organization noted: "Reactive social work practice is also about what's fast is best and ... when I look at some offices where the caseloads are literally between twenty-five and forty, I don't know where the room is for proactive, thoughtful, efficient practice ... I know of practice where the social workers don't know their clients and that's really scary."

Many MCFD social workers cite the extensive "system demands" as a factor in the excessive workload. The number of recording requirements, their complexity, and the time involved in their completion has grown in recent years. One MCFD practitioner estimated that an intake recording that used to take fifteen minutes now takes two to three hours. Practitioners estimate that paperwork requirements have doubled or tripled. The amount of paperwork coupled with the size of the caseload means it is impossible for practitioners to meet policy requirements. Completing the paperwork would mean virtually no client contact. When there is an inability to manage the work, some tend towards self-blame:

Workload is a real issue for workers, and even yesterday I was talking to one of my co-workers and she said she wasn't sleeping at night and she and [her] files are not getting along, and I said to her, "It's a workload issue" ... She says, "Like, should I even be in this profession?" And I said, "Of course." I said, "Don't doubt yourself." I said, "It's because of the workload you can't be the social worker you want to be" ... It's very difficult to meet the expectations of the ministry and still be able to have time to work with your clients.

According to one practitioner, the consequence of the many organizational changes at MCFD was "a huge turnover of staff." It seemed that the hiring of new staff couldn't keep up with the rate of attrition.[8] Although the rate of staff turnover has always been an issue for child protection services, the increased workload demands placed on practitioners and the lack of personnel have created a negative cycle in which "you don't have enough workers and you can't get them trained fast enough so you're burning out the other workers that are there so they end up leaving."

In one northern office there were five positions but only two practitioners at any one time. An MCFD practitioner, working in that office, commented: "Oddly enough ... after five months I was the senior full-time worker within the office." Another, at an intake office in a regional town centre where staff turnover is also frequent, commented: "That's pretty scary that you're the senior worker in under two, two and half years." Workload and staff turnover are significant issues at the ministry, but the emphasis practitioners now place on paperwork has several origins. New requirements flow from the development of legislation, policy, and computer systems, but the system also sends messages of reprisal and blame to its workers. This creates added pressure to complete all the "system demands" by paying more attention to paperwork. One MCFD supervisor described it as follows: "A lot of it is paranoia, you know, I don't want to dismiss it, to say that there aren't some real concerns, and I think that there are, I think a lot of it is the politics of the job ... I understand that but I don't think it should ever direct our practice." At the same time, this supervisor acknowledged that "it's hard, after a period of time, that you don't sort of incorporate that into your practice."

In general, the organizational atmosphere at the ministry is one of constant change, heavy workloads, extensive paperwork requirements, and fear of reprisal and blame. MCFD practitioners, with one exception,

---

8   The Personnel Division of the BC Ministry of Children and Family Development reports a staff turnover rate of 11.5 percent for the 1999-2000 fiscal year for social program officers in child protection positions. This provincial average may conceal a higher turnover rate among child protection practitioners in rural and/or northern areas.

did not describe receiving any support from management for creative intervention, nor did they speak about receiving any respect from management for their work. There were no indications that a climate of open dialogue, debate, and disagreement regarding practice was tolerated or encouraged.

Aboriginal Organizations

In comparison to the MCFD, organizational life in Aboriginal child welfare organizations appears to the practitioner to be relatively unproblematic. In many organizations practitioners receive respect from management, and there is an open dialogue about practice as well as a freedom to disagree. There is a sense of evolutionary newness that accompanies organizational life and, with it, a freedom to create, experiment, and innovate. There is no map to dictate what an Aboriginal child welfare organization should be, and one Aboriginal practitioner described it as a "pioneer process": "There's no map, I mean there is a map that doesn't belong to us, but there is no map in how do you create an Aboriginal child welfare agency? How do you keep kids safe? How do you deal with generational issues of pain? How do you deal with a history and reality of oppression and create new places for people to be? ... It's pioneering and you kind of make a map and then you find out that you are going in the wrong direction so you turn a different direction."

There is a climate of mutual respect between practitioners and managers, about which one Aboriginal practitioner commented: "Well, authority ain't coming down in a big way. It's the respect that's building up." Another explained it as follows: "It's just so basic, that you respect people, who they are, where they are at and there is a concern that comes in, but you work with them like they are people." And another characterized the organization as "a relaxed sort of agency where you go with your band and whatever your band believes."

There is also freedom for disagreement. One Aboriginal practitioner described a disagreement with a manager over "ministry style": "The ministry style was you don't sit down [and] waste your time doing all those circles ... and I'm coming back and saying, 'No, we're doing circles.' And then we would get into this big argument about who's right and who's wrong and I'd get fired more than once already and I said, 'Well you can't fire me.[9] You got to go to the board.' So there's a whole pile of that. Finally, we got it ironed out, [the manager's] at a spot where

---

9 "Circles" refer to family circles in which an intervention plan is developed with the participation of extended family members.

he respects [the band's] decision. It's not coming down like authority, it's the respect." A non-Aboriginal social worker working in an Aboriginal organization described decision making that involved "six or seven counsellors, five or six counsellors and the chief, and it's seven people making a decision and, like, they debate, they don't all agree ... And another nice thing about it is, if a decision is made and it wasn't the right decision or something backfired ... you can get back in there and get the decision reversed or a different decision ... the following week sort of thing ... so in a way it's more flexible and more accommodating."

Although Aboriginal organizations are significantly smaller than the BC Ministry of Children and Family Development, another difference is that some Aboriginal organizations define themselves as "learning organizations." One Aboriginal supervisor stressed that staff need to work in a climate where they can evaluate practice and learn from mistakes; therefore, she emphasizes a climate of safety and respect. It is important that staff "feel secure and confident about the job that they're doing and are learning through the process. And when they feel either personally criticized or professionally criticized and/or attacked by the evaluation component of the ministry then I have a responsibility and the chief and council have a responsibility to go: Oh, no." This supervisor's response indicates the challenge facing Aboriginal organizations – to ensure cultural autonomy in child protection while defining themselves as different from the MCFD.

Most struggle, tension, and challenge occur through attempts to distinguish the practice of Aboriginal organizations from that found at the MCFD. Sometimes the struggle is expressed in relation to policy, sometimes in relation to external review, and sometimes in relation to the constraints of available funding. One Aboriginal practitioner described the struggle as "continually doing the battle of not recreating the ministry on-reserve." In another Aboriginal organization a practitioner commented: "I think a lot of people, when they first thought that they were going to have this program as their own Native program, thought it would be different than what it is, and I think a lot of them are angry about it because they do perceive this as a branch of the ministry. [This is] because we are mandated under the Family and Children Services Act and so, although we try and maybe incorporate some of the Native teachings into it, when it comes right down to it, that's what we're living by and that ... [is a] ... very white piece of legislation."

An Aboriginal practitioner in another organization described the struggle to be different from the MCFD:

I think when it first started out it was very policy-oriented. The ministry was really pushing their style onto us. They had a worker right from the ministry. What do you call the big guy – that sits there and directs everything? Director, I guess, he was here, helping us starting our own, and his style was being projected upon us and I felt very uncomfortable with that and I'd bring his style to the community, the community would feel uncomfortable with it, so there is this great big tension there for a while. Basically, we had [to] grind out our differences. That's the director's style, it's not the band's style and we invited him up to see our community and hear our ways and how to do it and he refused. So he did send other workers out to come view our style, and they still sort of, "Well, yeah, we hear you, we see you, but this is what we want, this is how it is to be done." So the chief just said, "Well, here's the door. Get out."

In both practitioners' commentaries and in earlier commentaries about ensuring that staff feel secure and confident, one can see that political intervention on the part of chiefs and councils is necessary to ensure the freedom of an Aboriginal organization to practice in a way consistent with cultural values and traditions.

Aboriginal social workers in Aboriginal organizations express a different understanding of the power issues in child protection than do MCFD practitioners. One described the power relations of child protection as "an extension of colonialism and oppression, you know the power is in the hands of the judges and the social workers and everybody else but the family and the children."

Another spoke about it this way:

Authority, to Native people, Aboriginal people, is something that they can't deal with or they have a really difficult time dealing with because the government, in what they have done, the government right now, that's what they have done in the past, basically, had done it in a way where Aboriginal [people] do not have any choice, none whatsoever, to the point of removing children without even the parents' awareness. Sexual abuse, physical abuse, verbal abuse, cultural abuse, all of those things have been practised with Aboriginal people, and so therefore ... if you practice authoritarianism with them, it is not going to work. It may work to their advantage of getting kids out of the home, but anything further has just been totally destroyed ... the tactic could be changed from using authority to using, more like workability, and respect, and developing a good relationship.

This Aboriginal practitioner suggested that a historical understanding of the exercise of power on the part of the federal and provincial governments is essential to understanding the exercise of power in child protection practice today. The elements of authority and compulsion in practice are viewed as unworkable and need to be replaced by relationship building and respect. To describe the importance of non-authoritarian practice, an Aboriginal practitioner made an implicit contrast between MCFD practice and the practice of Aboriginal organizations: "We don't just jump in and say, 'You do this, this, this and this in order to get your kids back' ... if we would go into a home and start dictating how they need to raise their children, what they need to provide, and if they don't, then [we'd] remove the kids. I feel that would be oppressing them because we wouldn't allow them to have the power as parents. We would be taking the power away from them." All of these practitioners described the importance of minimizing the power differential in child protection practice and emphasizing respect and cooperation in order to ensure a child's safety.

Workload, caseload, paperwork, or "system demands" are not frequent topics of conversation among Aboriginal practitioners in Aboriginal organizations. This may be because the caseload in some Aboriginal organizations is significantly less than are those at the MCFD. The supervisor in one Aboriginal organization described the caseload as being between fifteen to twenty per worker, and only one Aboriginal practitioner had a comment to make about it: "If our loads get heavy then we look at them and we adjust ... I have noticed a lot of change in our caseloads ... our workloads are pretty heavy and our director and board have just hired five more staff so we will be able to ease off and not be so overloaded." One explained the difference between paperwork and system demands in an Aboriginal organization and those in the MCFD as a difference in the approach to practice: "If we were to go to court with the number of cases that each one of us is managing ... let's say, you know, a case a week or something like that ... our staff would be busy in paperwork. They wouldn't be able to be out there meeting families in the communities, doing home visits, and connecting with children."

Interestingly, two non-Aboriginal social workers in an Aboriginal organization spoke about workload in ways that were similar to how MCFD practitioners spoke of it. One acknowledged that there was less paperwork here than at the ministry: "Talking to my ministry friends that work for the ministry, and their paperwork there, they just don't have time to spend with their clients, and it's a lot worse there than it is here. And, you know, so much time is just spent doing paperwork that you don't have time to even really get to know your clients."

Another non-Aboriginal practitioner, when she was required to cover the caseload of two full-time practitioners for an eight-month period, described herself as "dancing as fast as I can" in order to manage fifty-two cases. She talked about how she felt humiliated and undervalued due to her inability to manage the workload. One senses in this discourse the pain, anguish, turmoil, and self-blame more characteristic of practitioners at the MCFD. It raises questions about whether the respectful positive climate in some Aboriginal organizations is a function of a smaller caseload rather than of the organization's size or culture.

Practitioners in both the MCFD and Aboriginal organizations stressed the importance of providing support to one another in the work environment, and they both described specific strategies such as "buddying up" on difficult cases. At times, an immediate supervisor's words or actions made a difference to practice. Those who are supervisors often described themselves as shielding practitioners from the "politics of practice," "reframing" it, or advocating against its intrusion into practice. One Aboriginal supervisor talked about the importance of taking a political stand against the MCFD's intrusion into practice in their organization. At one Aboriginal organization practitioners talked enthusiastically about the organization's "self-care" policy. Others in Aboriginal organizations talked enthusiastically about self-evaluation, learning from practice, creativity, and growth. These ideas are absent from the description MCFD practitioners provided of their organization. With one exception, MCFD practitioners did not describe management support for their practice, saying that only the team leader (the first-level supervisor) provided such support.

7
The Community Context

With our community ... everyone knows us, and they know the
job we do, so the respect is there. The trust is there.

> – An Aboriginal social worker in an Aboriginal
> organization

The importance of community-based intervention to effective child
protection practice has been known for some time (Fuchs 1995;
MacDonald 1997; Wharf 2002), but there is little understanding about
how child protection practitioners think about community in practice.
More particularly, when the community is a minority within the dominant society and the practitioner is a member of the dominant society,
how is "community" represented in the practitioner's thinking? When
the practitioner belongs to the minority community is it represented
differently? This chapter describes how geography influences practice
as well as how the status of being an outsider or insider in a community
affects one's practice. It also outlines five distinct ways in which practitioners think about the Aboriginal community.

Geography of Practice
Practitioners live in a variety of community contexts ranging from isolated reserve communities to regional town centres. The context in which
practice occurs for some is circumscribed within a three-kilometre radius of the office. Others practise within a series of small communities
found within an eight-hour driving radius from the office along gravel
roads. Some communities are accessible only by air, whereas others require a combination of air and road travel. The different relationships
to practice imposed by geography affect the way practitioners view the

"community" as well as the way the community understands child protection practice.

When practitioners and community members live and work in close proximity, the possibility of reciprocity in child protection is enhanced. Informal, non-crisis-oriented interactions are possible, as is described by this Aboriginal practitioner: "We have very much an open door policy, although, you know, we try to schedule appointments and stuff, they never work, people are always popping in, and I think that's really good, and people are coming in, they're asking why we're doing what we're doing and asking us to stand behind our decisions and ... not only questioning how do we do the work that we do but giving direction as to where we should be going." A Ministry of Children and Family Development practitioner in a small community confirmed this sense of reciprocity: "We even got to the point where families themselves would be phoning and identifying when they felt they needed services or when they'd need respite or they were feeling that they were slipping and they wanted to come up with a plan ahead of time, and they felt comfortable enough phoning us and talking to us directly." If the practitioner is a member of the community, then the sense of reciprocity is almost taken for granted, as this Aboriginal practitioner in an Aboriginal organization reported: "In the community we know everyone; we don't have to introduce ourselves. We go in, we know what the background is, we know the history ... we go into the home, we know the family, we work out a plan ... With our community ... everyone knows us, and they know the job we do, so the respect is there. The trust is there."

When practitioners and community members live far from each other, a level of social distance and formality enters the practitioner-community relationship. To the community, the practitioner is the distant outsider who appears as the external "other" to complete an investigation and to determine whether a child is in need of protection. When the practitioner "goes in" for a short period of time, the community tends to view her as a temporary visitor: "A lot of time you'll hear comments from the community, "Well, oh yeah, here they come, flying in, flying out.'"

The focus of work is the completion of a task – often the assessment of a child's safety and the negotiation of an alternate care arrangement. But when the time allotted for the community visit is one-half to one day little time remains for relationship development. The possibility of reciprocity in the community-practitioner relationship is much lower when the focus of practice is an investigation to determine a child's safety and removal (usually outside the community) to ensure safety.

When a practitioner resides in the community a different kind of child protection relationship is possible. While the practitioner knows community members and is visible in the community, this visibility brings with it a loss of personal privacy. The life of the practitioner is increasingly lived "in a glass bubble" or "fishbowl" and the distinction between a public/professional life and a private/personal life becomes blurred. Life is lived with the community's full knowledge, and this heightened visibility creates stresses and demands of its own.

Aboriginal practitioners who live and work in their communities of origin described opportunities for supportive informal intervention outside the office, along with the possibility of bringing their lifelong knowledge of the persons in question to the interaction. But the lack of anonymity places demands on the practitioner to engage in a lifestyle that conforms to community norms and is also congruent with professional practice. An Aboriginal practitioner described it this way: "Everything we do here is basically seen by the communities. We are like in a fish bowl, you know, the lifestyle we live in and outside the office people see. It has an impact, and I think that is also why we are looking at the type of lifestyles people have after hours. If they continue to go and 'party hardy' with some of their clients, that doesn't sit well with who we are as an agency, and come Monday morning I have to deal with that family."

One MCFD practitioner in a small community described his glass bubble experience in a similar way: "You're working even when you're in the grocery store. You're working if you're walking down the street. You're perceived as working, you're known as the social worker to the town and your actions reflect on the work that you do." The loss of anonymity in small communities creates opportunities for a greater level of reciprocity with regard to community life as well as with regard to the protection of children, but it also brings with it a loss of privacy. Furthermore, it can bring a strong sense of isolation for practitioners who are "in but not of" the community, and it can be a contributing factor to the high turnover of staff in isolated communities.

Community as Victim

Some practitioners represent the community as a victim in child protection. They see a relationship of powerless dependency upon the state and view their practice as reinforcing the community's victimization. They see a lack of community interest or participation in child protection decision making, with neither community leaders nor community members taking identifiable responsibility for children's welfare. A high level of internal community disorganization may exist, and this translates into an absence of support services and alternate caregivers in the community. One community member may use the intervention of an external child protection practitioner as a threat against another member – perhaps as an expression of lateral violence. Within the community, child protection is seen as a practice conducted by outsiders who investigate and remove children when safety is at risk. In this representation, practitioners have minimal relationships with the community; the community doesn't participate in child protection and has no identifiable role. The condition of victimization is recreated for the community each time a social worker parachutes into a community, makes a brief assessment, and leaves with all the children at risk. This form of practice often reactivates the image of the sixties scoop in the mind of the community. One MCFD practitioner commented: "You're going into these small Aboriginal communities and removing their children, you know. I don't like doing that, but you're also setting up or perpetuating something that has occurred for generations so the relationship that you're forming, well you're not forming a relationship, all you're doing is antagonizing what relationship may be there ... it's just like a continuation of the sixties scoop ... You'd get a call, say in a more disorganized community ... [that] a child's at risk, you go in and investigate. There would be very little involvement from community leaders, resource personnel that might be in the community such as a teacher or nurse or alcohol drug counsellor, and you'd be left to your own devices basically to plan for the child." With an absence of community-based resources, the child is deemed at risk, and the practitioner sees no alternative but to remove the child from the community.

Community as Adversary
Some practitioners represent communities as adversaries in child protection. They perceive the community to be closed to outsiders, including the child protection practitioner, and an adversarial relationship with child protection intervention exists. Usually this is expressed as anger at the BC MCFD and is manifested in a confrontation with its representatives. A minimal level of reciprocity with the child protection practitioner exists, and there is a formal relationship with the community for the completion of investigation, removal, and alternative placement tasks. There are few opportunities to establish working relationships. When the community is represented as an adversary, the practitioner

may serve as a lightening rod for the community's anger at child protection removals. An Aboriginal practitioner employed at MCFD described walking onto a reserve in a community that was not her own:
"There is a family that I have gone to on-reserve, it's just almost the
same, 'You're coming here to take the kids.' When I took the white
social worker to the reserve ... they said, 'You're not allowed on the reserve.' And I thought, 'Holy Cow,' but we were able to calm them down
and let them know why we were there."

An MCFD practitioner described her experience as follows: "When I
worked up north, it was a clear understanding ... that you did not go
onto the reserve unless you were invited, and when they invited us it
was for a protection concern and it always ended up as a result of a
removal. We weren't ever able to put in family supports or child care
workers or whatever."

Sometimes, the confrontation becomes politicized, as one MCFD practitioner described:

> When we do come out there ... some homes may say, "No, you're not
> allowed in." "You've got to go get the chief or whatever." And then
> depending upon the family, if they have political pull or not it will
> depend upon whether or not the chief actually supports us and helps
> us or if he says, "No, you can't, I'm making some phone calls." And
> then it goes from there. Some families it depends upon who you are on
> the reserves. Some of the bands don't care at all about them, you can
> do whatever with them, go and investigate, but if there's some politi-
> cal pull, it takes a lot with the lawyers and all that to get anywhere
> near the children and parents ... in some cases they'll go up the higher
> ranks and then we have to bow out and it becomes a big political mess
> rather than just going through the investigation. They get a lot of the
> higher Aboriginals involved, our management gets involved and a lot
> [of] times people higher up may not know the actual what's going on
> ... it just gets stuck up in politics rather than where it should be down
> below.

At its more politicized levels, the adversarial confrontation involves the
police and the media.

Community as Participant
Some practitioners represent communities as participants in the protection of children. At its most minimal level, this is expressed when community members take responsibility for reporting child protection

concerns to an Aboriginal child welfare organization or the MCFD. One MCFD practitioner said that this occurs once one gains the trust of the community: "The calls we were receiving to investigate increased over the two years that I was there, so that's also, to me, saying there is an increase in trust." The community becomes a participant in child protection when social workers consult with the community members when assessing situations and planning interventions. Sometimes this occurs through informal conversations with band leaders, the band social development worker, teachers, nurses, or daycare workers. An Aboriginal practitioner described her approach this way: "If I was going into a community I would phone and say, 'Well, who do I need to speak to about this? I want to get some information on this, and I am going to be coming out there in a couple of days, who do I need to touch base with?'"

At other times consultation with the community is more formal and takes place through a case conference. Although the community is involved in child protection, responsibility rests largely with the formal agency. Still, one can see the beginning of a reciprocal relationship. Reciprocity in child protection practice can also be expressed through community initiative to find or create alternate care resources. According to one MCFD practitioner: "In some of the Aboriginal communities, there's a lot more use of extended family in times of crisis. There was, I mean, [a] lot of people were drinking, there was an acknowledgment that usually there was somebody who was sober enough and able enough to look out for the kids ... There was somewhere for the kids to go or some means of protecting those kids ... We involved a lot of our people in the community in what we were doing."

Community as Partner
Practitioners represent some communities as partners, thus suggesting mutual responsibility for child protection and a reciprocal relationship based on mutual respect. Child protection intervention is acknowledged to have an effect on the entire community: "Because the family relationships are so intertwined and connected and strong in this community, we know that the work that we do has a rippling effect throughout the community." Social workers make conscious efforts to share decision making with the community: "We were going to follow through on what we said we were going to do, that our planning involved the bands, involved extended family, if the family wanted that to happen, and we'd involve the school in the planning. So these types of things would take place and the input was valued and it was appreciated and

... if at all possible, if we had any way possible of implementing it, we would do so."

Another characteristic of the partnership is that members of the community contact the agency at non-crisis times to discuss child protection issues: "We have also had teachers phone us, just to say, you know, I think this family needs some support here, they need a visit from your office." Sometimes children and youth contact the agency directly to make their needs known:

We have had kids come in here and say, "Mom and Dad are drinking. They are fighting. There is no food. I am scared; I don't want to go home." They are feeling safe enough to come in here and tell us that and so we would say, "OK, we will help, where do you want to be?" ... We had a seventeen-year-old come in and state that, "My Mom has been drinking for the past week. She parties and stuff. I need places to go and rest where there is no alcohol and no drugs." So we say, "OK, where do you want to be?" She says, "Well, I want to be out of the community ... where I can get some quiet and some rest." That is what we try and give them.

When a partnership exists, the agency and community share responsibility for child protection and cooperate in such endeavours as creating new childcare resources. An Aboriginal practitioner in an Aboriginal organization commented:

Before we place children in there to ensure that they are going to be safe and taken care [of] and not abused and used while they're in their home ... we also get feedback from community members. Like we usually go through the band social worker, and check with them or if they have ... child welfare committees or social development committees, we'll ask them if they would support this home as a resource because it is going to be within their community and they will be best to know whether or not that would be a good place for the children to be in.

Some communities have developed committee structures to enable them to have an ongoing role in child protection. One Aboriginal practitioner described a committee and its relationship to an Aboriginal child welfare organization as follows: "They have a child welfare committee ... we have been meeting with them a month at a time. You know, once per month in which they reviewed all of their cases that were ongoing with us, as well as the bands GFA [guardian financial assistance] to find out if there are some issues, who is doing it and what needs to be done and, you know, what recommendations could we make." Here there is clearly a reciprocal relationship between the community and the agency to ensure the protection of children.

Community as Protector

Some practitioners represent the community as the principal protector of children, with external child protection agencies playing a minimal to non-existent role. This representation is most often expressed by Aboriginal practitioners, and it may recreate the Aboriginal community's approach to childcare before child welfare legislation was introduced. One Aboriginal practitioner summed it up this way: "Traditionally, it wasn't uncommon for other members of the community to look after your kids, and basically that's all that we're doing now." Responsibility for children's welfare is a collective responsibility, and community members intervene to create alternative care arrangements for children as needed. Grandparents, aunts, and uncles are recognized as playing significant childcare roles. An Aboriginal practitioner described this as follows:

> Long ago our community was always community-orientated. We were always, you know, I guess a community. Our connections are there. We know everyone, we're related. We help out ... We always knew how to look after our children, our extended family would come in, the grandparents would come in. It always happened, I mean the community got together and said, "Hey, we have a problem here. Our aunt over here needs a break from her children. Can someone in the family take over?" That happened. We didn't need a child welfare act and all that stuff.

A non-Aboriginal MCFD practitioner confirmed this by describing how a community intervenes to protect children when the parents are unable to do so:

> Some of those families ... still have a far stronger traditional sense, so a number of things happen when they see unseemly behaviour or inappropriate behaviour. Mom and Dad are drinking, Mom and Dad are allowing a sexual abuser in the home, they will speak to them because that's the role of the matriarch or the chief ... they'll have a talk with them. "Ah, you are not behaving properly, you need to do this. This is your job." And if the parents don't respond, they'll take the kids and I'll

hear of it later. They'll say, "Oh, by the way, we have John and Jessie's kids now, in case you are looking they're here. And they're not getting them back until they straighten out." And you know, the funny thing, John and Jessie never say boo. They don't go to court. They don't phone the cops, they don't say peep, you know, they go, "Oh, okay," and either they keep drinking or they sober up real fast, but that's a strong family doing its traditional role – child protection.

These representations of the community's significance to child protection imply a range of relationships between practitioners and communities. At times, the relationship is determined by the community's openness to collaboration. At other times, it is determined by the availability of support services, the distance the practitioner needs to travel, or the practitioner's own vision of what constitutes good child protection practice. However, there is no clear association between the different representations of the community and the practitioner's culture or organizational auspices. It may be that the practitioner's own vision of practice significantly influences the relationship with the community. If the practitioner values community participation and has an understanding of the community and a commitment to community involvement, then a different community-practitioner relationship becomes possible.

8
Visions, Explanations, and Knowledge for Practice

> When we provide service to Christopher who's seven, okay,
> we are providing service to Christopher and his parents and his
> cousins and his aunts and uncles and his grandparents. That's
> what our hope is; that the work we do has a systemic impact.
>
> – Director of an Aboriginal child welfare
>   organization

This chapter examines three interrelated practice dimensions. It explores the practitioner's vision of her work in order to describe the ideals, purposes, values, and philosophies that inform practice. Next it discusses explanations of practice in order to determine the reasons for intervention with Aboriginal families. It explores how practitioners explain the causes of abuse and neglect in Aboriginal communities and the reasons they provide for their intervention. Finally, it describes meaningful knowledge for practice from the practitioner's point of view. Visions, explanations, and knowledge arise from the reflective analysis practitioners provide of their day-to-day work. This takes place within a historical, sociopolitical, organizational, and community context. The aim of this chapter is to describe distinct social representations of child protection practice by identifying the ideas, systems of interpretation, and guides for action that particular groups of practitioners employ in order to make sense of their work.[10]

The Practitioner's Vision
Practitioners state that "ensuring children's safety" is the common goal

---

[10] For a fuller discussion of the social representations perspective, which is the theoretical perspective informing this book, see Appendix 1.

of practice, and they anchor their description of practice ideals in four concepts: the legislation, the child, the family, and the community. Sometimes they describe their practice vision through only one concept. At times a second concept becomes visible, with one being in the foreground and the other being in the background. Sometimes one concept is juxtaposed against another in apparent equilibrium, whereas at other times several co-exist, with a subtle shading of priority among them. Each relationship suggests a different conceptual structure with regard to practice ideals. The relationships between these concepts, although complex, provide us with a way of differentiating one practice representation from another.

Child protection legislation is the point from which some Ministry of Children and Family Development practitioners explained their work: "Basically there's a series of laws that have evolved provincially and in all the provinces designed to deal with the issue of protecting the province's children from what's defined as abuse at the time, and I'm enacted, I guess, or empowered to just check to make sure that those laws or statutes are being followed, and if they're not that some intervention is taking place to assist the children who may be at risk ... Basically that's what it's about ... keeping the kids safe." This practitioner described societal sanctions for child protection practice; however, by citing the legislation to explain the purpose of child protection, he implied a regulatory or law enforcement dimension to the work. Another practitioner described her work more bluntly as being a "kiddie cop."

Some MCFD practitioners focused on the child's needs when describing practice ideals: "I'm here to make sure kids are safe ... making sure kids are safe, but also helping families if I can." This practitioner, and the next one to be quoted, recognized the child's family but almost as an afterthought: "Being involved with children, making sure that they're safe and even dealing with families in general, just ... to get them back on track, there as a support, whatever it took." The child is prominent in these responses and, although she obviously has some relationship to the family, the work is clearly child-oriented: "I think that the nature of child protection is to ensure the safety of the child, the ongoing safety of that child, and their well-being and to try and develop services and hook them up with services or do something ... within the family that's going to ensure that that occurs. I try and stay fairly focused on the child." A child-oriented focus raises questions about the family's significance to the practitioner's vision of practice. One MCFD practitioner argued that focusing on the child does not mean that family relationships are not important – even when a removal is necessary: "It's important to have a family contact ... I still think they should have some contact with their natural family." While these practitioners believe in "being focused on the child," this raises questions about the place of the family. Is it an afterthought, a background factor, or non-existent?

The significance practitioners give the family in relation to the child varies considerably in their description of practice ideals. One MCFD practitioner argued:

I cannot split child from family. A child is born to a family, even if the family is only a mother, and family is an integral part of that child and so I can't split the two ... You know, even if a child is a permanent ward and there is no family, there is a whole family in that kid's heart and in that kid's mind and that kid is working through the issue of family throughout the time in care and into their adult life and [they] revisit it again and again and again. I can't separate child from family.

As can be seen, this practitioner gives considerable significance to the child's family, as does the following MCFD practitioner:

Well, when I talk to children about who I am and what I do, I explain that I try and work with children and families so that [the] family can be a safe place for children to grow up in, and that a lot of my work involves helping families do what they need to do to become better able to do that, and sometimes that involves other people having to come in and be part of the family network for that child in order to make sure that they're safe and can grow and their well-being is protected.

The family's significance to child protection is evident in this practitioner's discourse, but, interestingly, the child's removal from the family is not discussed. The family was also important to this Aboriginal MCFD practitioner: "I explain to them that we work with families and children ... and explaining to them ... just the whole thing about the principles, the guiding principles that we have, in which the parents have the primary responsibility for their children, and ... we would try to support that as much as possible ... and when children are at risk we do have to intervene and what we try to do is to get families to resolve it."

Both these practitioners emphasized working with the family rather than removing the child. But others who emphasized the family also

acknowledged that "keeping children safe" was the foundation of practice, as is indicated by this MCFD practitioner: "The purpose of my work
is to support families, to support families and protect children in situations where their families aren't able to."

A non-Aboriginal practitioner in an Aboriginal organization provided
a similar description: "I think what we do is to try and ensure that families have the kind of support they need to give safe and life-enhancing
care to their children, and the primary thing that we do is try to ensure
that those children are safe, so I mean those two things – we try to offer
support but our first concern is to make sure that children are safe."
These visions of practice emphasize supporting the family, but this is
juxtaposed with an understanding that protecting the child is also important, and this includes, if necessary, removing her/him from the family. These visions of practice clearly place the child within a family
context.

Differences in the Meaning of Child-Centred Practice

Children can be removed from the family due to an absence of support
services, work volume, and policy-driven practice; however, sometimes
removing a child from the family becomes elevated to an ideal – child-
centred practice. One MCFD practitioner described the tendency to remove children as part of a "messianic complex" among "baby social
workers": "They are going to save these children from their nasty parents." In these situations, the practitioner juxtaposes the child with the
family in her representation of practice ideals. For example, practice is
child-centred when the practitioner protects the child from bad parents.
This emphasis on the child, in contrast to an emphasis on the family,
constitutes a major difference between practitioners: "I just see two main
differences, the ones that really are defending children and see them as
separate or separable from their family context, and those that really
totally want to just work with the whole family and try and make it
happen."

To some, child-centred practice implies separating the child from the
family. But to one Aboriginal MCFD practitioner it meant focusing on
the child's needs: "You have to be thorough ... get as much information
as you can ... This child focus thing, when it comes to protection, it
really helps me, like when I have to make a decision ... to focus on the
child's needs rather than just the parents, you know ... the safety is the
most important thing." Being child-focused, to this practitioner, means
thinking about the child's needs but not necessarily removing the child
from the family. To another MCFD practitioner it meant that the child

has a right to a childhood as well as to being protected: "Often in families there's a role reversal, and the child is parenting the parent and they need to be a kid and I strongly believe in that."

The emphasis on the child in the representation of practice ideals is subject to interpretation. The child can be viewed as having a greater moral claim to intervention than the family, to having greater value than the family, or to having a greater claim to thorough needs analysis than the family. However, unlike family-oriented practitioners, child-oriented practitioners do not identify the sources of their thinking about practice in their representation of practice ideals.

Sources of a Family-Oriented Practice Vision

Practitioners who emphasize the family in their practice ideals described the idea as originating through family experience, knowledge of the foster care system, professional education, and community feedback. These perspectives are illustrated as follows:

Family experience: "I come from a really large family so I know that all the problems in our family were always dealt with by our families. Maybe not always the best way, but we always took care of each other, you know, and in a small community it is there, if you look hard enough." (a female MCFD practitioner)

Knowledge of the foster care system: "When I first started with the ministry I think I really wanted to help, but if I were to bring a child into care, I didn't have the long-term realities of what happens when kids come into care and frequent moves and foster homes and other kids with behaviour issues in the home and all those kinds of complicated things that, you know, that you need to see people having to deal with and experience to know that the alternative you provide the family better be as good as or better not be ... worse than what they're leaving." (a male MCFD practitioner)

Professional education: "The few workers that we worked with, within the ministry, couldn't see that. Like ... after they had gone back to school, they said, 'You know what I learned was this family system stuff, you know.' And we said, 'Yeah, okay.' I guess without being so conscious of it, that is the way we have been operating here, as we operate from that system of family, and if we are working with a [person] who doesn't have a family here, we try to become that person's family." (Aboriginal practitioner in an Aboriginal organization)

Community feedback: "I just learned it through experience basically. You know people would say to me, 'Hey, you just come and talk to ... Why do you just deal with the parents here? There's a big family here, we all care about these kids.'" (Non-Aboriginal practitioner in an Aboriginal organization)

These examples suggest that a variety of experiences – whether acquired through the family, professional practice, professional education, or community feedback – influence some practitioners to move towards a family-oriented vision of practice.

Child Protection in Aboriginal Communities

A different discourse becomes apparent when child protection ideals are discussed with Aboriginal practitioners, especially when the protection of Aboriginal children is being described. One Aboriginal practitioner joked when asked what child protection work is about and said its purpose is "to take children away." Another responded: "My husband used to say I abduct children."

Although these statements preceded a more serious response, they portray the intensity of the child protection experience in Aboriginal communities. In its title, one book refers to "the Abduction of First Nations Children" (Fournier and Crey 1997), and several Aboriginal practitioners refer to the sixties scoop when they discuss their work. A non-Aboriginal practitioner saw her practice as "still sharing the legacy of the missionary." Child protection ideals have a more powerful meaning to Aboriginal practitioners than can be conveyed in the simple phrase "to protect children and support families," which is often used among non-Aboriginal practitioners. When Aboriginal practitioners describe community reaction to their work, they reinforce the importance of defining practice as distinct from the historical legacy. One Aboriginal practitioner remembered the initial community reaction to her work: "I can recall when I first started working with ___ going to a home on the reserve, and I didn't know that this family was drinking. I walked into the home, they were drinking, and when they seen me coming, they sent the kids to run up the mountains. That was the image they had of social workers." Another Aboriginal practitioner remembered people saying, "Oh, you are one of those baby snatchers," and a third described reaction to the removal of Aboriginal children in Quesnel: "When they went in there and just apprehended all those kids, that really brought up that old feeling ... Yes, scoop kids. That ... you're just coming in to scoop kids and you don't even care, you don't understand."

The practice ideals of Aboriginal practitioners stand in sharp contrast to this negative imagery:

I see what I did in the area of child welfare as doing something, I think, for the good of the community and the children because I think that ... everyone in the community is responsible for those children. Traditionally, that's the way it was, and to some extent we still maintain that value within our community, and I just seen my role in some ways as an extension of that ... I can remember having a major insight one day why it was so important to do the type of work that I was doing there, like it wasn't important just for the child or the parents, it was important for communities as a whole, and that often the work that I did was the catalyst for healing of the individual child in the community.

Aboriginal practitioners tend to describe their ideals broadly. For example, the Aboriginal practitioner above described her purpose as "to empower children and families," whereas another said: "At the end of the day, making sure that kids are safe and that families are intact and that we're actually about promoting health and creating change and that, as a First Nations agency, we're also not only a role model to this community but a role model to other agencies." This practitioner described Aboriginal child welfare as: "Reclaiming or giving voice to traditional values and practices, to honouring and recognizing and celebrating children and families in the community ... health promotion ... it's more proactive in nature ... and it's much more holistic ... We're always trying to be the big picture thinkers."

These broad perspectives pertaining to practice ideals include "community." As one Aboriginal practitioner explained: "Our whole job ... right now is working with children in ensuring their safety and their well-being within our communities ... I become involved with the child and the parents and so when I work with children and parents in the Native community, I work specifically with the child, the parents, the siblings and it extends out to aunties, uncles, grandma, grandpas, community members. It is a very large area that I work in when a child protection issue comes forward to me."

Another Aboriginal practitioner sketched a model of the child's relationship to the community: "If we look at the model of ... how the community operates, at the centre of that model is the child and then the family and then the extended family and the community." She described her practice as follows: "When we provide service to Christopher, who's seven, okay, we are providing service to Christopher and his parents and his cousins and his aunts and uncles and his grand-parents. That's what our hope is – that the work we do has a systemic impact because of the relationships in your family since you're seven. And the community, because the family relationships are so intertwined and connected and strong in this community, that we know that the work that we do has a rippling effect throughout the community." To another Aboriginal practitioner the ripple effect is long-term: "When these kids grow up we're going to be the elders, sitting in a home or wherever and they're going to be the ones working ... the product of what type of decisions that we make will show in about twenty years, with these children, when they grow up and they start getting their education and start working." The quality of care elders can expect in the future is intertwined with the quality of care children are receiving today. As can be seen, the practice ideals of Aboriginal practitioners in Aboriginal organizations are generally broad, and while they focus on the child within the context of the family and community, their think-ing extends beyond this to the reciprocity involved in care-giving be-tween generations.

Broad practice ideals are not restricted to Aboriginal practitioners, as is shown by the description of practice provided by this non-Aboriginal practitioner in an Aboriginal organization: "I think child protection meets immediate protection of children in need that need to be made safe, but it's expanding off of that, it's the hope that you can support a family enough to care for its own children and you know, those chil-dren are safe, if possible, and then trying to help families to grow and then Aboriginal communities often means working with the whole com-munity to raise awareness to make programs or help people to be re-sponsible for children."

It is clear that ensuring children's safety and well-being is the founda-tion of practice; however, in their description of practice ideals, some emphasize legislation while others emphasize the child, the family, and the community. To some MCFD practitioners the execution of a legisla-tive mandate is central to their understanding of the ideals of practice, whereas to others the child is central. Some MCFD practitioners ac-knowledge the child's family but place it in the background, whereas other MCFD and Aboriginal practitioners emphasize the family. Some Aboriginal practitioners begin with the child, move on to the family, and then to the community.

Although the interrelationship of practice ideals is complex, three distinct visions of practice are suggested. The first vision places the child clearly within the legislative mandate of child protection and envisions meeting her/his needs through legislation and state-provided resources. The second vision places the child within the family and attempts to meet the child's needs, if at all possible, through the resources of the family. The third vision places the child at the centre of the family and community and attempts to meet her/his needs through the resources of both. The first vision is most often found among MCFD practitioners, whereas the second is found across the entire range of practitioners. The third vision is often found among Aboriginal practitioners in Aboriginal organizations, but it is also found among non-Aboriginal practitioners in Aboriginal organizations as well as at the MCFD. Although differences exist, a simple conclusion about the relationship between practice vision and culture, or practice vision and organizational auspices, is not possible.

Explanations for Practice

Child protection workers intervene in families' lives when a child's safety is at risk and there are indications of possible abuse and neglect. But how do practitioners make sense of the need for their intervention? How do they explain the underlying causes and conditions that prompt it? Interpretations of the causes of abuse and neglect in Aboriginal communities, and the needs, issues, problems, and conditions to which intervention is addressed, are the focus of this section and are more generally described as the social condition dimension to practice.[11] In general, these ideas are somewhat elusive as practitioners in everyday life spend little time explaining or interpreting the need for intervention. But such ideas exist, often only partially formulated, under the surface of practitioners' thought.

I found three prominent themes in how practitioners think about the social condition. For some the dominant theme is the inability to parent, with poverty, alcoholism, violence, and parental residential school experiences being contributing factors. For others the dominant theme is loss of identity, to which dependency and powerlessness are contributing factors. Alcoholism, violence, and the inability to parent are viewed as symptoms of this broader malaise. For yet others the dominant theme is colonization, which entails relations of subordination that result in poverty, alcoholism, violence, dependency, loss of identity, and the inability to parent.

---

11 See Appendix 1 for a fuller description of the significance of the social condition dimension to the theoretical framework of this book.

The Inability to Parent

Aboriginal and non-Aboriginal practitioners explain the need for intervention by describing parents who do not adequately care for their children. It is a concrete, obvious, and accessible way to interpret the social condition. Sometimes explanations are framed in terms of the parent's immaturity or unmet needs: "[It is] really tough when you have parents who themselves are so limited or so needy that they can't perceive their kids' needs." They are unable to put their own needs aside to respond effectively to their child. In such situations young children are a particular concern, and practitioners describe parents as needing parenting skills. But the inability to parent can also be viewed as having to do with the parents' choice of discipline (especially the use of physical discipline) or their failure to provide adequate supervision: "I spoke to this seven-year-old who cared for his four-year-old sister, alone, on a regular basis. I mean he knew how to cook Kraft dinner ... he was being the adult, taking care of the younger sibling."

Although parental inability to provide adequate care is the most immediate condition that prompts intervention, in determining how this inability develops, particularly with regard to Aboriginal parents, one is frequently led to historical factors such as the residential schools. One Aboriginal practitioner described it this way: "Our parents were in residential schools and they didn't know how to be parents because they never saw their parents. It's those needs ... It's those days that we are looking at now because whatever happened way back then has produced these parents that only know how to act like a nun or priest, and so they are teaching their kids with the same whip and same lack of closeness."

Another Aboriginal practitioner explained a parent's lack of ability to bond with her child by saying, "She had gone when she was young into residential school, so she didn't have ... the ability to know that it was okay to hug your child, to praise a child rather than only when the child does something wrong ... you beat them." A third Aboriginal practitioner described the effects of residential school abuse on men's ability to parent: "If Native males at a young age were sexually abused and physically abused, had no parental support or contact for maybe anywhere from like five to ten years of their life, so they have no parenting skills. They are angry because of what happened to them, they bottle it up, they drink excessively, they act out the abuse that they received in residential school, you know ... They were taught that the way to parent [is] the way they were parented and it's the only model they have."

Understanding the residential school experience and its lingering effects on former students once they have become parents led some practitioners to identify an intergenerational dimension to parenting ability: children who live with abuse, neglect, violence, and addiction often become parents who are abusive, neglectful, violent, and addicted. In the words of one MCFD practitioner: "Parents who were abused as kids, you know, they haven't done their growing up, they are taking it out on the kids, they don't know it, so they either deny it outright or they minimize it horrifically, which keeps them away from doing the hard, dirty, messy, painful work of personal introspection and rebuilding."

There are a number of intergenerational factors that influence parenting capacity, including negative experiences of being parented oneself, parental lack of personal healing, extensive parental use of alcohol in early adulthood, and the ongoing lack of sobriety on the part of some family members. One practitioner described a family as follows: "[The] auntie in that family has been sober for about five years, maybe eight years, [but] she is having a heck of a time, because the mom and a couple of her siblings keep trying to bring her back down again to where they are at." Addiction, abuse, and violence are frequently described as intergenerational issues that influence the ability to parent. However, there can also be an intergenerational dimension to child protection intervention, as one MCFD practitioner indicated: "In this community there's a few generational ... families that have been involved with the ministry for generation after generation after generation, you know, they just can't seem to get off the system."

When practitioners begin to generally reflect upon the conditions that precipitate child protection intervention, they talk about violence, poverty, dependency, powerlessness, and loss of identity. Sometimes they relate these conditions to the inability to parent; others, as is seen in the next section, relate it to loss of identity.

Loss of Identity
Some interpret the social condition by introducing the concept of dependency. Practitioners provide numerous examples of government-funded programs that have led to communities becoming "really too dependent on the welfare system":

They had a brand new home and they were under the DIA [Department of Indian Affairs] and they couldn't do anything in their home for I think it was twenty years or something. Anything they had to do, had to get permission, I mean, that's their home, they should be able to do what they wanted ...

Then there's housing ... they've got people coming in and saying "My door knob is broken." "Okay, so go out and get it fixed, you know, and whatever" or "My sink faucet is dripping." So they will get somebody to fix it ... Those are simple things, can be taught, there's no reason for it, for somebody to always go in and [be] fixing their faucet.

Although dependency is viewed as a consequence of government programs, others see it as part of a more general feeling of powerlessness. One non-Aboriginal practitioner explained powerlessness as a consequence of social change: "Aboriginal people don't live in traditional societies any more and they ... don't have power over the societies they do live in, so we're dealing with symptoms of a structural disease." Dependency and powerlessness, though, can be viewed as part of a more general theme confronting Aboriginal peoples – the loss of identity that results from the loss of language, culture, religion, economic independence, and participation in family and community life. However, Aboriginal practitioners do not directly explain the abuse and neglect of Aboriginal children as a consequence of identity loss. Some of them explain the powerlessness, dependency, and loss of identity in Aboriginal communities as being due to colonization. The abuse and neglect of Aboriginal children is seen as a consequence of the loss of cultural autonomy that occurred due to the imposition of external systems of power and control. Both the residential school and the child welfare system create dependency, powerlessness, and loss of identity as they are part of the process of colonization, which subordinates Aboriginal children and families to the cultural norms of the dominant society.

Loss of identity affects Aboriginal communities in a variety of ways. With teenagers, it may result in an inability to "respect themselves or others" due to a lack of cultural knowledge. And of course racism contributes to the loss of a positive childhood identity. As one Aboriginal practitioner put it: "When I was growing up I was called Spear Chuck or a Wagon Burner, you know, Scout, whatever, you know, it was very derogatory regarding the fact that I'm Native and stuff but, and like at first it hurt me, and I would go home in tears."

The loss of a positive Aboriginal identity may also be the result of the parents having greater respect for "fair" members of the family. As one Aboriginal practitioner explained: "My grandfather was non-Native, so the fairer we were in our family, the more better you were. So therefore, the more Native you showed, you weren't as highly respected."

Those who grew up in the non-Aboriginal child welfare system lost not only family and community relationships but also a positive cultural identity as an Aboriginal person. At the heart of these experiences of loss of culture and identity is the imposition of a system of laws, policies, and values on Aboriginal people by the non-Aboriginal society. Although one Aboriginal practitioner saw a clash between the child welfare system and "our way of living," other Aboriginal practitioners were even more forceful. To one, the power involved in child protection is external to the community: "We received our power to do our job from outside of our communities, from outside our people. It comes from [the] ministry, with ministry guidelines, ministry direction, and, you know, the laws that we work within are theirs not ours, not our peoples'." To another, the child protection system was "an extension of colonialism and oppression": "There was no need for that, the children were cared for within the community, and it is an extension of colonialism and oppression. You know, the power is in the hands of the judges and the social workers and everybody else but the family and the children involved in the situation. There's that assumption that all First Nations people can't care for their children."

The losses for Aboriginal peoples encompass land, language, culture, religion, family and community life, and economic independence. These losses contribute to feelings of powerlessness, dependence, and the loss of positive personal and cultural identity.

Colonization

Another explanation for child protection intervention is to view it as the long-term consequence of colonization. Loss of cultural identity, powerlessness, and dependency are merely steps along the way to the inability to parent. The child welfare system is viewed as both an instrument of colonization and a contributor to the loss of cultural identity, to powerlessness, and to the creation of dependency. That it exists to ensure children's safety and to protect them from harm is problematic for both Aboriginal and non-Aboriginal practitioners. As one MCFD practitioner said: "When you look at the percentage of First Nations children in foster care, historically, and where they have been placed, and how they have been raised, I mean, it's contributed to genocide as much as residential schools have, in some respects." Another MCFD practitioner commented: "It has been used as an assimilation tool by the government for many, many, many years."

Practitioners described the negative effects of the child welfare system on Aboriginal children, but they did not clarify whether these were historical or contemporary. However, they did argue that little has changed, which suggests that problematic aspects of the child welfare system as it relates to dependency, powerlessness, and the loss of cultural identity have not been eliminated. As far as one Aboriginal practitioner is concerned, British Columbia's new Child, Family, and Community Services Act still imposes non-Aboriginal standards on Aboriginal communities and does not recognize Aboriginal ways of protecting children. In fact, it runs the risk of continuing the abuse of Aboriginal children through child welfare: "It does not speak to how First Nations govern themselves or their family or their children. So we're looking at legislation that is imposed on an Aboriginal child welfare system. Primarily Aboriginal child welfare is a family responsibility, it isn't the responsibility of a system. So when we look at developing and maintaining our agencies, the big risk is that historically we come from a place where we have experienced oppression and abuse by what was called child protection."

A non-Aboriginal MCFD practitioner argued that his colleagues at the MCFD do not understand that there are differences between the culture, values, and childcare practices involved in the care of Aboriginal children and those involved in the care of white children: "Often times white social workers haven't a clue of who they're dealing with and how that person thinks and operates, you know. Like we know enough now to know that the cultures work differently, but we don't get exhaustive training in that ... We're still not training social workers in appreciating how Native families raise kids, and what that means in terms of child protection."

To this practitioner, one of the differences between the cultures is that

> Native families are far more laissez-faire about their kids. Why? Well because when you grew up in [a reserve community] every second person who stuck their head out the window was your auntie or your grandma or your cousin. So of course you played on the streets with your buddies because there wasn't a lot of cars around and everybody knew you and half of those people who knew you had a special responsibility for your safety and half of those people made no bones whatever about correcting your behaviour in the community if you got out of line. You know you would get reported on real fast to your mom, if they didn't deal with you directly themselves. So that was the way kids were raised ... so then that family moves to [town] and they are still laissez-faire with their kids but nobody on the street knows them ... So,

you know, we look at that and we think, "Oh oh, bad parenting." Well, no, culturally they haven't adapted yet ... their parenting style doesn't work as well as it used to because they're in a different environment.

Other non-Aboriginal MCFD practitioners provided similar comments, all of which pointed to the fact that cultural differences in childcare are generally unacknowledged by non-Aboriginal social workers, and there is little being done to change this.

From the preceding discussion we can see that, although child protection intervention is viewed as being fundamentally about the inability to parent, the determination of the latter can be the result of a worker's inability to recognize cultural differences in parenting. When legislation, policy, and procedures to protect children are vested in the dominant society, then culture-blind intervention is possible, if not probable, with regard to Aboriginal families. Child protection practitioners recognize the authority vested in their position, but they differ remarkably in how they exercise this power. The creation and implementation of interventions without the parents' participation, let alone the participation of the extended family or community, occurs today, and it results in the continuation of the cycle of domination and subordination. With regard to this cycle, it is the memory of the residential school that casts the longest shadow over Aboriginal communities.

Legacy of the Residential Schools
Our understanding of the social condition of Aboriginal peoples is incomplete without a discussion of the residential school era and its significance. At some point most practitioners described the impact of the residential schools on families, communities, and children. Whether it was a parent's inability to hug a child, addiction, violence, depression, dependency, powerlessness, loss of language, loss of culture, and/or loss of self-respect, the residential school experience is at the heart of the conditions that create child abuse and neglect in Aboriginal communities today. It is ever-present in a variety of ways, and one of these is the experience of shame. One Aboriginal practitioner described her mother as follows:

She was shamed and whipped ... she would speak her language and she got whipped for it, disciplined, they went out one day, they were allowed to be out on the grounds at the residential school, and her and a few other girls went out and they ate Saskatoons and because they ate Saskatoons, which is a Native food, they were disciplined ... They stayed there twelve months of the year and basically what the whole residential school program was ... it's almost like reprogramming them, taking away their foods, their language, their beliefs, their values. They weren't allowed to pray in the Native way, or they had to pray the Catholic way, and a lot of physical abuse, a lot of sexual abuse ... My mother, she was seventy-six, and whenever I tried to get her to speak her language – because I wanted to learn – and every time, it got so, got a little easier for her, but she would speak in some of her words, but she would laugh and she would get shy, and the shame that came around that held.

Others remembered their fear: "It's like a body memory of being in residential school and getting caught at maybe stealing vegetables out of the pantry, whatever, it will bring back that body memory and it's more devastating to that person ... because they're bringing up a body memory maybe that was thirty, forty, fifty years ago or so." The shadow of the residential school hangs over Aboriginal communities today and informs practitioners' explanations of the causes of abuse and neglect.

Knowledge for Practice

Social work education emphasizes integrating theory with practice in order to develop a framework that guides practice. Education about research emphasizes integrating knowledge into practice in order to develop a scientific, or knowledge-based, approach to social work. Although these assertions have guided social work education at the baccalaureate level for many years, there has been little systematic exploration of the ways in which practitioners utilize knowledge – whether as theory or research findings – in their day-to-day practice. This section explores this theme by identifying areas of knowledge that practitioners found helpful, by describing the knowledge they needed in order to work well in complex situations, and by identifying references to social science concepts found in their discourse about practice.

Practitioners' Use of Scientific Theory

Practitioners conceptualize their thoughts, interpret social reality, and explain practice by referring to scientific theories. In their discourses about child protection we find elements of psychological, sociological, and political theories. I found no difference between Aboriginal and non-Aboriginal practitioners' use of theory, with one exception: some Aboriginal practitioners make reference to colonialism but no non-Aboriginal practitioners do so. Scientific theories are incorporated in a variety of ways in order to orient thinking and to make sense of child protection practice. For example, a psychological theory like Maslow's hierarchy of needs (Maslow 1968) helped one Aboriginal practitioner focus on a client's basic needs: "I think the real basics of human needs, like the need to belong, the need to be loved, the need to be safe, the need to be fed, sheltered, those basic needs are, of course, what we look at."

Some incorporate more than one theory in order to conceptualize their practice. For example, one MCFD practitioner referred to attachment theory in order to describe key themes of child protection: "The fundamental themes in child protection work are separation and loss and attachment and family. You can't have separation or loss unless you have two aspects. You have got 'child,' you have got 'family,' and they are so interwoven." However, this practitioner also described the family in ways that suggest that family systems theory influenced her thinking about practice:

> I cannot separate the child and the family and I will work with both, with both parts of a family – the child in whom we have the protection concerns, and whoever the rest of the family is. They are both my clients, both parts of the system ... I have lived with those [foster] children through all of their ages and stages of development. And all along the children have to rediscover, with me, what it means for them to be foster children, to be in a family, a birth family, a family of origin. And the kids are always redefining and reinterpreting that to themselves.

It is the reference to "both parts of the system" and to the "family or origin" that is suggestive of family systems theory.

Another Aboriginal practitioner incorporated concepts from both attachment theory and colonization theory. In order to describe a family member, she said, "She didn't seem to have the bonding"; however, in order to describe the needed redesign of the child protection curriculum for Aboriginal social workers, she said: "We ... decided on what it is we felt we needed in those training programs ... So we said, 'Well, first off we need to start from where it started – colonialism.' So that is what we did ... Then the next one, the next phase, residential schools. That was the next impact. They need to know that, residential schools and the sixties scoop. They need to have the background in that to know where a lot of these parents are coming from. Where they are at and why their kids are the way they are. So they need to have that as a foundation."

The foregoing practitioner referred to "colonialism," but it appears in her discourse as a "theoretical fragment." This suggests an awareness of theories of colonization which explain successive waves of European domination in Canada. This practitioner stressed its importance as foundational knowledge; however, the extent to which she understands the theory is not clear. Another Aboriginal practitioner used attachment theory in order to critique the politicization of child protection practice in some Aboriginal communities: "There is a band here in BC that has partial delegation, does not have full delegation, who, a couple of years ago, repatriated all of their kids from all over the province and actually from the United States. Brought the kids back home into the community, violated and traumatized those children by abusing the attachments and bonds that they and the families [had] ... and then brought them home to [a] community with no resources or infrastructure. That's reactive social work practice and that's about a political agenda superseding the best interests of children." This practitioner also used colonization theory to describe the impact of the new BC child welfare legislation on Aboriginal communities: "We're looking at legislation that is imposed on an Aboriginal child welfare system ... historically; we come from a place where we have experienced oppression and abuse by what was called child protection."

These examples suggest that practitioners use theories from different disciplines – political science, sociology, and psychology – in order to interpret child protection practice. At times, they refer obliquely to the results of social science research: "You know, research shows when you study the deaths of children, very often it is the first incident [of abuse] that has ever happened."

One practitioner referred to research findings when describing Aboriginal children being placed in non-Aboriginal homes: "I remember my first supervisor, up north, was really pro-family and was always very aware of the research on the Aboriginal children in non-Native homes and the difficulties they faced and was very supportive of the communities, and that really influenced a lot of what I did after."

Whether it was the supervisor's practice approach, rather than the ability to cite current research (or the integration of the two), that influenced this practitioner is unclear, but it is an example of how research results are incorporated into thinking about practice. Some practitioners appeared to be influenced by research findings, but the relative infrequency of research references in the interview data suggests that these are in a minority. Only one practitioner made a citation-like reference to social work theory: "I don't know if you're familiar with Anderson,

Joseph Anderson's model, you know, kind of a stage where with every client you should be working with the individual, advocating some way for the community and dealing with some macro issues and part of what happens I think is that we're getting more and more limited in terms of being able to advocate for anything internally and even externally, you know."

Although all the practitioners interviewed had a social work education, the overall influence of social work theory on child protection practice appears to be minimal. Just two practitioners made a passing reference to a theoretical model, implying that it had significance to their practice. One MCFD practitioner commented: "I've had countless discussions with my staff around that approach to problem solving. For example, looking at the harm reduction model in terms of alcohol and drug, and incorporating that with child protection." The second discussed intervention in an Aboriginal community through a "community health model" and commented on the implications of this for community work.

Sometimes the way a practitioner used a particular concept suggested it guided and structured practice thinking. A non-Aboriginal practitioner referred to dependency: "I think a lot of the communities they become really too dependent on the welfare system, which to me is a real tragedy." Dependency suggests colonization theory, but this practitioner did not make that link. In general, practitioners provided little evidence to suggest that their decision making is informed by scientific research. Some practitioners described the family system's significance to the child, as well as the importance of maintaining the child's connection to the family, but it is usually not evident that these ideas have a basis in family systems theory or child welfare research. It is possible that scientific theory and research findings do influence practitioners' thinking in indirect ways. From time to time fragments of theory and research appear to be incorporated into practitioners' thinking without necessarily creating an empirical or theoretical foundation to practice. However, to describe child protection practice as guided by theory or as informed by research would not reflect the practitioner's reality. In fact, one MCFD practitioner argued that child protection practice is "common sense" and is not informed by theory: "Areas of knowledge ... probably I just don't think about it. Um, it's funny actually because there's all sorts of things you do and when you read about different theories and stuff you think, 'Oh yeah.' Well, you know you think about that, but you don't do it, you don't think about it when you are doing it ... I think a lot of the stuff we do in this job is basic common sense ... I mean there are always the theories and stuff you learned in school but I have never consciously applied them."

By contrast, an Aboriginal practitioner articulated a vision of theory-guided practice: "Well, I think I need to have some basis in theory. I do, I really do believe in that because how do you know where you are going with a client if you don't have some basis in theory? Like how do you know how to proceed with that client? So to me that's first and foremost, you need to have some knowledge, right ... how do you explain rights to clients, if you don't have some basis in legal knowledge around the Young Offenders Act, maybe the child welfare legislation." This practitioner suggested that knowledge of social work practice theory, as well as relevant legislation, is important for practice. But the lack of a substantive empirical or theoretical foundation for child protection practice raises another issue. If scientific theory or knowledge does not inform practice, then what does? The answer practitioners provide is: experience. Whether constituted as practice wisdom, practical knowledge, or awareness of practice contradictions, the practitioner's own experience appears to significantly influence her decision making.

Practice Wisdom

A challenging case, a move to a new community, a life transition, or a supervisor's words of counsel are experiences that prompt the occurrence of new learning. Each has the potential to produce new guides for practice. Such newly acquired knowledge can be concrete and practical, as this MCFD practitioner described in discussing a personal safety strategy:

> There was this one time I was afraid a kid was going to freeze because it was forty below and the cabin was heated with wood and I couldn't see smoke coming out and was afraid the fire was out and the parents were in town drinking, so I axed the door. Wham. I embarrassed myself completely because there was a fifteen-year-old there looking after this kid, but she didn't answer the door so I opened it for her. Anyway, in explaining this to my supervisor the next day, his first question was, "You have to stand to the side when you do that 'cause if you don't and they shoot through the door, you're dead." I went, "Oh, okay."

Experience teaches some MCFD practitioners to be more assertive, to take "less bullshit," and to be more aggressive in their practice. It teaches some Aboriginal practitioners in Aboriginal organizations to act with more assurance, to put more trust in the community, and to be more of a risk-taker. At times, experience teaches the importance of redefining success so as to be able to accept little (or later) recognition for one's work. At other times, it teaches that life's changes can be a foundation for practice changes. Becoming a parent, for one Aboriginal practitioner, led to erring on the side of removing children in order to ensure their safety: "When in doubt, I am more likely to move to that place of taking kids into our care without all the information when it all happens. Which isn't about reactive practice, but it's about, I think, that my own personal commitment to the safety of children is a lot stronger."

A male MCFD practitioner described the impact of parenting on his practice: "I think once you have children, you know, you see that in a very different frame of mind, and certainly I'm a single parent so having a lot more compassion and understanding for single parents and seeing and understanding their level of frustration, their level of stress, I'm a lot more compassionate."

Moving to an Aboriginal community as a non-Aboriginal person also creates changes in practice. Several non-Aboriginal practitioners described changing their practice in order to emphasize building relationships with the extended family and community so as to include them in decision making. One MCFD practitioner explained:

I think what really struck me was how much I didn't know. I mean I knew my job in terms of child protection, I knew the legislation, I knew the policy, I knew how to operate within that very narrow definition of what my job was, but when you look at that in a much broader context of those people in their community, in their homes, and couple that with some of the historical stuff about where they've come from, what's happened to them, I really didn't know that much. I had to really change gears in looking at how I was going to work with these people, and most of what it was, was not per policy or per legislation, it was developing a relationship with these people and developing a relationship with the community.

Through experience, this practitioner and others acquired a new emphasis on the value of relationship building.

Practical Knowledge
Knowing the family, community, and culture is useful practical knowledge for child protection in Aboriginal communities. It is often acquired through developing relationships in practice, as an MCFD practitioner in an isolated community explained: "I typically know the family, and know of the family before I go and do an investigation. I've probably

talked to them in a store or on the side of the road. I know who they are and they know who I am, so there's a bit more of a relationship built instead of just showing up cold and not knowing this individual at all."

This practitioner and others stressed the importance of not only knowing the family but also of knowing the family history. Both Aboriginal and non-Aboriginal practitioners stressed the importance of knowing the community. As one MCFD practitioner explained:

> Each community has its own culture and belief systems and having to realize that I had to know that and know how this belief system impacted on how my work got done ... It was my responsibility as a social worker to learn about the different communities. Learn about their history and learn that, for example, ____ was the main centre for the residential school. That it was one of the last residential schools to leave the area ... So listening to the people that had been [there], and that were willing to talk to me about how that impacted on their lives and having that knowledge and utilizing that knowledge within my practice [was important].

An Aboriginal practitioner also stressed the importance of knowing the families in the community: "There are families that don't associate with certain family members and you have to be aware of that, so you have to know the history of the community." This practitioner described this knowledge in more detail: "When I go to any community here, there is only like a couple of people that I don't know. When I go to a house, I have a knowing of who they are. Who their parents are, or who their grandparents are ... We also had the connection of what their history is. Whether or not they were alcoholics or whether or not they were abusers or whether or not they were abused. So some of them, like I said if somebody were to examine my head with all the knowledge I have on families, it would be, you know, overwhelming."

Aboriginal practitioners have a particular ability to know the family and community because they often live in the community and know the culture. One Aboriginal practitioner stressed this when assessing a child's needs and comfort level with alternate caregivers: "With certain children they are used to eating wild meats, deer meat, moose meat, salmon and they're used to eating ... a lot of rice, a lot of potatoes and not the real fancy foods."

Both Aboriginal and non-Aboriginal practitioners acquire practical knowledge through the experience of living within a particular community or culture or through working with a particular family. Practitioners cite these experiences as the most powerful source of knowledge for their practice.

Disillusion and Contradiction

Awareness of contradictory realties and disillusion are other forms of knowledge that practitioners develop through experience. Their disillusionment comes from the limited policies, practices, and resources for child welfare. The inability of the foster care system to provide effective help to children, the inequities between Aboriginal and non-Aboriginal child welfare systems, the lack of changes resulting from reform processes, the unfairness of a judicial decision, and the level of politicization of practice are some "experiences of disillusion" to which practitioners refer. To them the ideals of practice stand in sharp contrast to the realities they know. Child protection practice aims to help families be a safe place for children, but families often experience intervention as the unwanted and intrusive violation of their privacy. There is an expectation that practitioners proceed cautiously and thoughtfully in investigative practice, but the workload and caseload demands often prevent this. There are increased demands and resources for practitioner accountability but no additional resources to meet the needs of children. Increased preventive services could reduce the number of children coming into care, but funding for prevention services is little to non-existent. Children in care often have a better standard of living than do children who are with their natural family, but the latter do not have the same resources available as do the former. Ensuring a child's safety often means taking the child into care, but alternate care does not ensure safety or well-being. An MCFD practitioner discussed this concern in more detail: "When I first started in the ministry I really wanted to help, but if I were to bring a child into care, I didn't have the long-term realities of what happens when kids come into care and frequent moves and foster homes and other kids with behaviour issues in the home and all those kind of complicated things that you need to see people having to deal with and experience to know that the alternatives you provide the family better be as good as or better, not be worse, than what they're leaving."

Practitioners have an exhaustive understanding of the contradictions within their practice reality. But the ways in they respond to this knowledge is unclear. Some may leave, others may narrow their vision, and still others may refocus their vision in order to find and practice the "art of the possible." The lack of knowledge about how practitioners resolve their crises of awareness needs further exploration.

Search for Language

A significant challenge for Aboriginal child welfare involves finding appropriate English words to describe Aboriginal ways of caring for children. The current language of child protection heightens the experience of contradictory practice realities for Aboriginal practitioners. One described the difficulty the community had understanding the application of child protection laws when they were first introduced: "Basically, the community just had no awareness at the time what social work meant, what child welfare or apprehension means. Like, those aren't words that we use in our language or in our ways. So, when someone comes and takes your child, it's sort of a family breakdown to us, but for someone to label it that was totally foreign." Another noted that: "When you talk to Aboriginal people across Canada and you ask them what the word is for protection in their community no nation has a word that says that ... The language around child welfare is primarily non-Native, and so when we're looking at what is Aboriginal child welfare, we need to look at what is the language and what is the system that we're buying into, and that we're not just duplicating the ministry system."

These practitioners underscore the challenge of finding the appropriate language with which to describe Aboriginal child welfare practice. In one community foster parents do not exist, but family caregivers do. An Aboriginal practitioner explained: "The reason we changed the phrase from 'foster parents' to 'caregiver' is we say they are not parents for these children, for any time, if it's one day or if it's two years, you know, these children do have parents."

Another community has a "child safety team," a phrase that describes an emphasis on the safety of children rather than on their protection. In these examples and others, there is a struggle to develop language to describe the reality of Aboriginal practice. To the Aboriginal practitioner, the language and practices of the dominant society's child protection system are inappropriate within the Aboriginal community. Yet the legislation and policy within which delegated child welfare services are created is non-Aboriginal. This creates a fundamental contradiction for the Aboriginal practitioner. On the one hand, the policy delegating child protection authority to Aboriginal communities appears to provide autonomy for Aboriginal peoples to care for children in culturally appropriate ways. However, the concepts, procedures, and rules within which such services are framed derive from the dominant society. Aboriginal communities know traditional ways of caring for children, but identifying such ways solely through the use of English concepts and language reduces and oversimplifies complex experiences. It also transforms such experiences into the categories and schemata of the dominant society and thus aids in the process of colonization. As part of reclaiming authority for child welfare, Aboriginal communities need to have their distinctive ways of caring for children recognized, and they also need appropriate language to discuss issues of importance.

9
Choices for Change

> One of the keys is the ability to form relationships, build relationships, and to, in a sense, have relationships with communities.
>
> – An Aboriginal social worker

Child protection is about assessing a child's risk of harm and developing a plan to ensure his or her safety, but in the process the practitioner confronts a number of choices. These involve how broadly to gather information about the child, how much emphasis to place on building trusting relationships, how to approach the use of power inherent in the position of child protection, and to what extent the family should be supported to ensure the child's safety. This chapter explores the choices at the heart of day-to-day decision making in child protection practice. It describes concrete actions and, more significantly, explores practitioners' thinking about the choices and alternatives involved in such actions. When Aboriginal children are considered, additional layers of complexity confront the practitioner. These include the historical legacies of a residential school system that began in the late nineteenth century and continued until the 1980s, as well as extensive foster care placements and adoptions of Aboriginal children into non-Aboriginal homes, that began in the 1950s and continue today. These legacies influence and inform the thinking of parents, communities, children, and social workers. Today, when a social worker meets an Aboriginal child or family to discuss child protection, this meeting may be an encounter between strangers from different cultures who have never met. It can also be an encounter between persons who share a culture, history, or community life, or strangers from different cultures who have developed a relationship of trust. The changing nature of this present encounter is informed by past decisions and involves a series of choices for the future of the child, family, and community.

Building Relationships

The image of child protection in the collective memory of Aboriginal peoples often consists of the massive forced separation of children from their families and communities by state social workers. As one Aboriginal social worker remembered: "They just filled the bus right up and took the kids out and just about every one of my relatives have been in foster care and I was very traumatized as a child, I never did forget my first cousin and her brothers. My first cousin was sitting on my grandmother's knee and Mrs. ____ came in, and I think there was another social worker with her or the police, I'm not sure, but literally dragged my cousin off of my grandmother and she was just kicking and screaming and didn't want to go."

This historical representation of practice features prominently today in the understanding Aboriginal peoples have of child protection practice. Each media story that suggests a child has been unjustly removed from its parents reinforces this understanding of practice. At the moment a child protection practitioner appears at the doorway of an Aboriginal home, an atmosphere of fear, distrust, and anger is unleashed. Based on historical experience as well as some present-day practice, there is an overwhelming fear that an encounter with a child protection social worker will result in the separation of a child from her/his parents, extended family, and community. Most practitioners I interviewed recognized that trust and credibility are integral to effective practice, and, to some, the challenge begins when one knocks at the door to assess a child's safety in the home. However, to others, the challenge begins when one enters the community for the first time. Building trust is viewed not only as interpersonal interaction with a child and parents but also as interaction with a community.

To build trust with a family the social worker needs to be open, respectful, and calm. Recognizing that the parents are going to be angry, hurt, upset, and volatile is part of the process, as is taking a non-directive approach. A non-Aboriginal social worker commented: "I often just come right out and ask, you know, 'What do you think is the best way we can approach this problem?' Because it is a very difficult thing, and in any situation you don't want to offend people, but especially when you're working with [the] First Nations community because they are very sensitive to white people coming on reserve, to child protection workers showing up with concerns about their kids."

While the historical experience with child protection informs the community's response to a practitioner, a social worker can also influence that response. This non-Aboriginal MCFD practitioner described being accepted in an Aboriginal community: "I was just patient. You know, you just kind of learned their ways, like you have to be very respectful. You wait for them to ask for your input, like you don't give them your input, you wait for them to ask, and ... I would say I was there two and a half months before they saw me as a worker rather than the white welfare, and it was just a really slow, slow process."

The challenge of building credibility involves dealing with not just the legacy of the sixties scoop but also with the legacy of the residential schools. As one non-Aboriginal practitioner commented: "I even hear it said, 'Well, you're just like the residential schools, you're trying to tell us what to do.' And even when it's not vocalized it is there, you know, that we're an interfering outside agency [that] doesn't share their experience, letting them know how they're supposed to live their lives."

Credibility for child protection practice needs to be constructed with community members in order to counter the historical legacy. It is less about formal assessments and safety plans and more about building reciprocal helping relationships with the members of a community to ensure the safety and well-being of children. One MCFD practitioner described the change in thinking about practice that this requires: "Going into these small isolated communities, you have to develop that relationship and that's primary ... It's more of who you are, what you are, and how long are you going to stay ... There was that mistrust, distrust, that occurred ... I really had to change gears in looking at how I was going to work with these people and most of what it was, was not per-policy or per-legislation, it was developing a relationship with these people and developing a relationship with the community." An Aboriginal practitioner in an Aboriginal organization echoed this: "One of the keys is the ability to form relationships, build relationships, and to, in a sense, have relationships with communities. And to be credible and to be visible in the community."

Forming relationships with communities is difficult when one is non-Aboriginal and from outside the community. The non-Aboriginal practitioner must bridge a cultural difference and a historical legacy through her personal credibility and ability to establish reciprocal working relationships. The process of building credibility begins by offering opportunities for involvement and decision making in child protection. One MCFD practitioner in a small, isolated Aboriginal community described a commitment he made: "If we were in a position where we would have to remove a child for the child's safety we would be doing our best to make sure that the child would stay within the community, to develop foster homes within the community, to try and build resources within the community ... So after we had gone in there a few times and worked, the community saw our effort in trying to develop foster homes and placing kids there and keeping kids within the community."

While credibility requires relationships in the community, it is enhanced when the practitioner is Aboriginal. At times, simply being an Aboriginal person who works for MCFD is an asset in building credibility with the Aboriginal community. An Aboriginal MCFD practitioner observed: "When I come knocking on the door, of course, there's the initial kind of defensiveness, whatever, but there seems to be kind of a slight barrier taken down when they see that it's me, because of the fact that I'm Indian as well, whereas I find that, say with another worker, the defence is up, you know, it stays up for quite a while, whereas a bit of it comes down if I go to the home."

Many spoke about building relationships with parents, the extended family, and the community, but others did not. Two Aboriginal social workers observed that, for some social workers, relationship building was secondary:

I find that some workers will come in [and] fix the problem, or they come up with a plan and the problem was fixed but there is no building relationships as much ...

The Ministry worker, one of the workers I worked with, we went out, did a home visit, she went in, this is the problem, this is what's gonna happen, this is my plans. I want you to obey this for the next three months and, well, God, like, how will they, what happened to getting to know the people?

Most practitioners quoted in *Protecting Aboriginal Children* see building trusting relationships as central to effective child protection practice, though they also observed instances when this was not a priority. To create trusting relationships, the practitioner must be calm, patient, open, responsive, respectful, and understand the parents, family, and community. The benefits of this are less intrusive intervention and family members who support the plans developed for the children.

Assessing a Child's Needs
The practitioner assesses a child's needs in order to determine whether a plan for that child's safety is needed. At this stage, practitioners gather

information from a range of people, but the key decision is whether to emphasize information gathered from community professionals or information gathered from extended family members. A non-Aboriginal practitioner in an Aboriginal organization described how, as a result of community feedback, her approach to assessment changed to include more family members: "Something that's taken me a while to learn is to not try and deal with a client just by himself but also go to his family, bring a family meeting together or talk to the head of the family. You know I've been scolded for that before, 'Why did you just, you know, do this without discussing it with, so and so is the head of our family.'" Being the head of the family is described as "an informal power position." People come to the head of the family and ask for advice.

When an Aboriginal practitioner is known by the extended family, a complaint about child neglect is viewed as an indirect request for help, as this Aboriginal practitioner described:

One of our workers, the way she goes in is with a calm approach saying, "Hi, this is who I am." They say, "Oh, I know who you are," sort of thing, and "This is what I do. This is part of my job. I am just following up here on a call that we got and I am here to come and to see what is happening here. If there is anything we can do for you." So rather than come in with this authority, we go there with information. Yes. We go there with information for them, like all of our services, if they are in need, and you know, if they are a single parent and we get a call stating that she is neglecting her child, she is leaving them for long periods of time, we'll catch up to the Mom and say, "Listen, are you needing a break? We know that, as a single parent, there, it's hard being a parent twenty-four hours a day, seven days a week and you know, twelve months of the year and that sort of thing, so our agency is here if you need some support for a break.

The assessment phase is a balancing act – balancing personal and child safety with relationship building, balancing respect with authority, and balancing being assertive with "not giving away" authority. In an isolated community, one practitioner described this process as she tried to ensure a child's safety without relinquishing her authority: "I was trying to ... get the family to solve their problem and I waited ... outside the house and they kept telling me, you know, someone would come out, every once in a while and tell me, swear at me and tell me to get lost and I just said, 'No, I am not leaving here until the children are out of this house and into a safe house. I'll see them into a safe house.' And they eventually did, they eventually did come out. I took them to a safe house and the police never did have to attend." Sometimes the challenge is to balance trusting the parents' ability to adequately care for their children with providing a response sufficient to MCFD policy requirements: "I'm always balancing between the comfort level in working with parents to keep that bottom line of their kids safety foremost in their minds or, let's say a little more upper in their minds, and then turning around and working within my ministry to make sure we don't snap every kid for whom we can't, you know, we can't make completely safe."

One tool to assist practitioners weigh the various factors influencing a child's safety is risk assessment technology. This was introduced in British Columbia about the time the interviews for this study were taking place, but it created another challenge for the practitioner. It resulted in yet another balancing act, as this MCFD practitioner described, particularly when one wants to use it in a "community inclusive" way: "We're seeing the community as the parent ... everybody in some way feels a connection to the child and it's important that they take part in raising that child and therefore they should take part in the decisions that relate to child protection ... So when we were doing risk assessments, I was very comfortable with [asking] 'Who would you like involved with the risk assessment?' when I was talking to parents, and a lot of times it would be grandmothers and uncles and aunts and extended family, and then we would work together on coming up with a safety plan. It would be a real group effort."

Another MCFD practitioner described a risk assessment process that begins with the risk assessment tool but evolves into a traditional house meeting:

Here's sort of an example of how I would try to do it. A couple drinking, being unfaithful to one another, leaving the kids in bad company while they both take turns drinking in town ... I'll call a risk assessment meeting. I'll do it in their community, I'll call the two sides of the family together and I'll ask [the Aboriginal organization] to do the invitation ... And then I present the issue. I just say, "I'm concerned about this couple." "This is what they are doing." "This is what it says to me as a social worker." I want and sometimes I do a fairly standard kind of risk assessment. I walk them through all the steps and get them to say "Yes" or "No" and rate them and stuff like that. And sometimes we do what's a far more traditional house meeting where they stand up and they make speeches. They are very oral people. They make speeches. They're basically speeches of support. "Listen John, I'm here for you, I know you are having a tough time now, and I'm here for you." Which basically means straighten out, you know, you're being offered help here buddy, take it. Sometimes what I'll do is I'll just leave the meeting. I'll get up and say, "With respect, I think this is now a family matter. I would like to hear the outcome, good-bye." Sometimes you find these wonderful uncles that sort of pop out of the woodwork at you and give you all sorts of options. First, they can step forward and volunteer to be restrictive foster care resources if that's what you need. They can [also] take the errant niece with three kids who's drinking aside, and give her bloody hell, and they know her far better than I do, you know, I mean I have my little day notes and my little intake reports and, you know, my formal bureaucratic ways of trying to get a read on this person ... They've known her since she was two. So, you know, they haul her aside and give her hell – or him as the case may be ... So that's a big part of the work. You look to see what kind of family is there and you use the family that's there.

Although some practitioners argue that the risk assessment tool is "clumsy," "culturally biased," and "adds to an already overburdened workload," practitioners must decide whether or not to use it.

Using Power

Practitioners recognize the power inherent in child protection, but they describe different approaches to its use. Some see the assessment phase as enabling families to build a sense of personal power. One way to accomplish this involves letting family members know that they can question the practitioner's decisions and contact a lawyer. An Aboriginal MCFD practitioner described her approach: "I want that person to realize that they have options, they have things that they can do, even if it's just to make themselves feel better, if they want to question my practice, that's okay because I feel stable enough and competent enough in what I do that I've done what I should be doing."

Central to some practitioners' work during the assessment phase is the process of assisting families to recognize that choices exist, that they have the ability to influence decisions. However, at times, when the imminent safety of a child is at risk or the practitioner's own safety is in question, police involvement is needed, and this creates an abrupt change in the equation of power. When there is a history of violence or alcohol use, practitioners are most likely to involve the police; but some involve the police simply because they do not know the family. When a practitioner knocks on the door accompanied by the police, there is a "big big change in the response," as one male MCFD practitioner described: "The police and the uniform and the authority, it's even more intrusive and more intimidating when they're going. So, I mean, for myself, as soon as I'm feeling comfortable, typically I'll let the police know that I'm okay and it's fine and then get them to go, so that calms things down."

Balancing the complexity of the power relationship in practice is an ongoing challenge. According to one practitioner: "I've never really met anyone that takes that authority too lightly and brings that big stick out of their pocket and threatens people with it." Yet according to another: "We have a worker that is well known for barging into houses, you know, without knocking." Yet another talked about the use of the "power button" – "that cockiness you see in some voices" when a social worker demands compliance by threatening the removal of a child. A fourth described a situation in which social workers and police circled a reserve with five or six police cars, presumably to overtly demonstrate the power of the child protection investigation. In general, Aboriginal practitioners report little use of the police in child protection investigations and talk about the power relationship differently than do non-Aboriginal practitioners. They recognize that the power invested in the role of the practitioner symbolizes how, with respect to child welfare, the Aboriginal community is controlled by the provincial legislation and authority. At the same time, Aboriginal practitioners recognize that the authoritarian history of the residential school era continues to influence child protection today. Communities, families, and children have lost a sense of personal power, and they need opportunities to regain this through collaborative decision making about childcare. A practice that is highly directive, bureaucratic, or rule-oriented recreates the power relationship of the residential school era and disempowers parents and communities. According to one Aboriginal practitioner: "We don't just jump in and say, 'You do this, this this and this' in order to get your children back ... We ask them what it is they need because they are the best ones to see where they are at and to know what they need."

Some Aboriginal practitioners renegotiate the power relationship in child protection through the use of voluntary care agreements rather than court intervention. An Aboriginal practitioner in an Aboriginal organization explained this choice as follows: "We would rather work with the parents ... providing services to support the parents while the children were in their homes rather than removing them ... We would work with the parents if the parents said, 'Well, I am in a place now where I really can't take care of my kids,' you know, we would work with that because that is where the parent is at."

Aboriginal practitioners recognize that family members or band leaders will sometimes use MCFD social workers as "the heavy stick" in order to influence other family members' childcare practices. One Aboriginal practitioner employed by MCFD described it this way: "Why they call me is because they want me to know about it and they want me to talk to one of their band members ... or one of their family members ... and they want me to say, 'This is the bottom line here, you do this,' and they want me to say 'I'll remove your children if you don't do this.' But I don't, I can't say that." Community members may try to recreate an authoritarian relationship by placing MCFD practitioners in the position of directing, threatening, and/or punishing parents, thus pushing them towards compliance.

When practitioners and community members know each other and have developed a relationship of trust and respect, the potential for the overt use of power in child protection practice decreases, as does the number of removals. When the family and the practitioner are strangers, it is more likely that the police will be involved and that children will be removed.

Supporting the Family

At the conclusion of the assessment phase, the practitioner's next steps are tied directly to the adequacy of support services and alternate caregivers available in the community. Practitioners describe a wide range of support services to assist families, but their availability and accessibility is the principal issue. When a child is deemed to be unsafe in a community that has no support services or identified caregivers, there is little choice but to remove her/him from the family and community. When support services are available and accessible, a practitioner can consider leaving the child with the parents and provide increased parental education, support, therapy, or supervision. In general, support services reduce the need for children to come into care. But in isolated communities, the absence of services sometimes means that practitioners take a child into care on a temporary basis in order to provide her/him with necessary services. An MCFD practitioner described this process in a small isolated community: "I would fly up on a given day and one of the elders would ask me if, or say, 'You know, I think this boy needs to be in care for a little while,' and us doing that, or even at the request of the chief, or even if it's not for purely sound reasons, you know, in terms of what we are required to do, we would do those things and bring kids into care and try to get them medical help that they wouldn't have up there, try to get them to see a specialist, eye doctors, things like that, for educational reasons, if the school wasn't functioning properly. For those kinds of things we would bring kids into care as well."

Improvising services sometimes means recognizing an informal caregiver within the community without the formality of a foster home placement. An MCFD practitioner commented: "In the smaller communities, you know, there's a lot of people who look after the kids and as long as that occurred I was fine with that and as long as there was involvement by the band to check up on them." However, in a climate of bureaucratic rule-oriented practice informal placements would be problematic. An MCFD practitioner described an informal care arrangement he wouldn't repeat today:

I remember responding to a call one night about some kids being unattended, and taking charge of these kids and placing them with a neighbour who was able to look after them, and that was the intent of the legislation. It was intended for me to act this way; however, what happened after that point is I placed with this neighbour and the parent returned looking for the kids sometime later and the neighbour, in turn, had called an extended family member who had come and driven from out of town to pick the kids up and, of course, the child's parents returned home, knew that I had taken charge, called us wanting to know where the kids were. I was responsible for those kids. I had no idea where they were because the neighbour had in turn called the relatives so I was left in a position where I don't know and ... that was a horrible position for the ministry, for myself, to be in, so those less intrusive measures now I don't do because ... there's a potential around complications that aren't spelled out.

The demand on practitioners to improvise resources, particularly in isolated communities, underscores the need for adequate support services. Some communities made it a priority to create alternate care resources, and, in one case, thirty-eight new foster homes were developed in less than four years. Increased support services in Aboriginal communities broaden the options available to the practitioner, enabling less intrusive child protection intervention. But a lack of on-reserve funding for such services, as well as the funding structure, is the heart of the problem. Funding is available for alternate care but not for family support services, and this creates a double standard for childcare in Aboriginal communities. The resources available to a child in care are greater than those available to the family. One Aboriginal practitioner observed: "If a child is in care and residing in a foster home and all of a sudden has a clothing allowance and a spending allowance and is in kick boxing and karate and swimming and when that kid returns home and the parents are living at the poverty line or below the poverty line, the parents can't meet those standards."

Removing Children

No decision in child protection practice is filled with more tension, uncertainty, political significance, and doubt than the decision to remove a child from the family. Ostensibly, a child is removed to stop or prevent harm from occurring. However, only in a minority of cases is the decision clear-cut. In the vast majority of situations, the decision is complex and is achieved by balancing a multiplicity of factors. Removals of children have particular significance to the Aboriginal community as they are rooted in the residential school era and memories of the sixties scoop. Awareness of the emotional damage that occurred to families and communities due to the loss resulting from these removals is the lived experience of many Aboriginal practitioners. However, to the non-Aboriginal practitioner as well, the removal of a child from the family has political significance. If the wrong decision is made, suspension without pay, a public inquiry, an internal review, and emotional trauma can be the practitioner's lived experience.

Making the decision to remove is simplified by the circumstances of some cases. One MCFD social worker described an "easy" removal in which she had to go out after-hours with the RCMP. There was a couple on a bus with an infant; the parents were very intoxicated and unable to take proper care of the baby. The passengers on the bus, according to the bus driver, were ready to kill the parents. The police took the intoxicated couple to the police station, and the practitioner removed the baby and placed it in foster care. This was a simple, clear-cut removal. But in most cases decision making is more complex, particularly when the quality of care the parent provides ranges from acceptable to unacceptable: "The less simple removals [are] the marginal parents, the ones who are right on the border line of what's acceptable community levels of childcare ... and sometimes the parents [are] above that level and sometimes they slip below the level, and there may be reports coming from different community members [saying], 'How can you leave that child with this family?' and you are always having to be monitoring the situation and constantly reassessing what the risk is to this child." Another MCFD practitioner echoed this theme:

We get to the real gray area of, well, it's sort of protection, there's some concerns, the family is kind of not really working with us, do we continue to try and plug in services, do we try and, how far do we force that issue, what do we do, do we back off completely and just close it and say, you know, we're no longer involved. We run a risk in doing that, if something blows up later on, which invariably it has happened, or do we keep them going and just sort of plug along? That's a much less extreme form of that, but the thinking is still down that same line because we're kind of worried, we're second guessing ourselves to some degree. If we pull out and don't do anything, have we crossed every bridge that we need to cross?

To one MCFD practitioner knowing when to remove a child involved being clear about your "bottom-line," which she explained as follows: "If you can go home at night and you know that kid's safe, right, if you still got something there, then look into it more and you may possibly have to remove." However, sometimes there is a lot more doubt and uncertainty about the decision to remove, and the practitioner begins to question herself: "Am I making the right decision by removing? ... Unless it's really obvious that there's abuse here, which the majority of times there isn't. So am I making the right decision?"

Part of the issue for some practitioners is that removing a child ignores the damage that can occur to families and children from that child being in care: "All that's looked at is the front-end problem. That is dealt with and the logistics of the long, ongoing issues that result are kind of ignored." Another practitioner from MCFD echoed this theme: "There are a lot of kids that are really resilient and they are better off in situations ... that are difficult and [should] be with their family ... But just because a family is in crisis, or just because a family's ability to cope is being really challenged, doesn't necessarily mean that the child would be better off somewhere else." These practitioners both suggested a cautious, conservative approach to removals, as did another Aboriginal practitioner:

[It was] very traumatizing for the kids and I think that contributed too to a lot of the alcoholism and stuff, for the kids that were taken away, a lot of suicides ... A lot of the kids, you know, their testimonies are that they were abused in the homes that they were placed in. They were the ones who have to do all the chores and the work around the house, while the foster parents' children didn't have to do anything. They were treated unfairly in a lot of the homes. Some of them were even beaten; some were sexually abused in the homes that they were put in. Definitely their culture wasn't upheld, so there wasn't just the separation from parent but community and self as far as who they are.

Decisions about removals are influenced by the ministry climate of "zero tolerance for children's deaths," summarized by an MCFD social worker as follows: "It's better to pull a kid and for it to be a mistake than to take the chance that this child might be at risk and work with the family." But one MCFD practitioner held another point of view: "No matter what I do, it is going to be questioned, and so I might as well do what I think is right in the depth of my soul because, in the end, someone is not going to like what I have done."

Deciding to remove is a complex decision influenced by the availability of resources, the organizational climate, the evidence, the child's needs, and the practitioner's vision of practice. When removals are discussed, MCFD practitioners have more to say than do Aboriginal practitioners in Aboriginal organizations. The latter have clearly observed removals in various capacities, but they rarely speak about them as an intervention strategy. It is clear that other strategies are preferred – voluntary care agreements, support services, and the use of the extended family and community. Removals become truly a last resort.

Working with Families and Communities
The ways in which child protection practitioners work on a day-to-day basis vary considerably. To some, intervention is a process of assessment and referral to outside services, whereas to others, it is a process of building family strengths and empowering parents to be the best they can. To others, it involves ensuring that the extended family and community are able to protect and effectively care for the child. When practitioners assess and refer, this is described as a "triage" approach to practice: "We get the intake and then we decide whether it's going to go here or whether it's going to go there or over somewhere else, but we don't really do the work ourselves ... to a large degree." Intervention is instrumental and leads to the provision of specific services intended to benefit the family. Support services such as a homemaker, family support worker, or childcare worker are introduced, or the child is removed from the family and/or community and placed with alternate caregivers.

Practitioners who start by building family strengths offer support, principally to the parents, in ways intended to build and maintain an open supportive relationship with the family. One Aboriginal practitioner described it in the following way: "I know, from my own parents the pain of where they are at, of trying to do the best they can, with what they have got and respecting that. You know, they have all good intentions of being the best parents they are with what they got, and at times it is just not enough, so rather than condoning that they don't have these skills, what I would do is I would say, 'Well, what if we en- hance the skills you do have?' and work from there." Practice focused on supporting the parents can mean offering concrete services such as a homemaker or respite care; however, just as important as the service is building a supportive relationship with the parents. In some communi- ties, support means offering a cultural service in order to teach "respon- sibility, respect and diligence" through activities such as participating in sweat lodges. In one community support is accomplished through a "family circle," as this Aboriginal practitioner described:

> The group got together and we talked about what we can do, and the group was all people who were from head families ... and it was a mix- ture of people, age level, like we had elders, some council members, the chief, we had some of the direct family members involved in the case, they were called in and we had some of the workers ... but each case was screened, based on what the call was and who's related and who isn't. We come together as a group and the case is disclosed and to- gether everyone decides, "Well, this is what I think," then the family has a chance to speak, and they usually say where they're coming from, what they are lacking, and plans are made from there.

In one community family circles had been operating for about eight years and could have as few as six or more than twenty participants. The person in question invites family members to the circle, but at times the chief and council ask for the participation of elders. The aim is a balanced circle with both family members and those who do not have a direct interest in the family. The practitioner provides an overview, and then allows the circle to discuss the situation and to reach a decision. When this occurs, the practitioner develops a contract with the family and helps carry it out.

In another community, a child welfare committee had a quasi-formal role similar to that of the family circle described above. The practitioner convened a family meeting and invited the person(s) in question as well as family members and members of the committee. The situation was discussed and a decision made. When MCFD practitioners described group processes used to support families, they usually referred to case conferences rather than to family circles or meetings. These are usually composed of the nuclear family, professionals, and community resource persons. At times, the nuclear family is not included and the case conference involves a discussion between the professionals involved in the child's life. In general, extended family members are not present.

There are also strategies that involve the community in child protection practice. These include community education about such topics as fetal alcohol effect or fetal alcohol syndrome, involving the community in creating alternative care resources for children in need, and/or public relations campaigns to inform the community about what child protection practitioners do. One MCFD practitioner described the rationale for a public relations campaign: "Lately ... people have ... not heard from the ministry's side of it. They see the one side, and they of course, they are going to believe it, and so they come up against us all the time with that side of it ... 'You're just going to come out and take our children.'" The presentation includes an explanation of the legislation, of the process of child protection practice, and of the steps taken before a removal. They have been given to both community groups and schools in the hope that they will change public perceptions of child protection, build credibility in the community, and develop effective working relationships.

Practitioners in Aboriginal organizations describe other strategies focused on the community. In one, there is an annual "honouring children" celebration:

> We recognize our children all year long but this is where we do it in public when we make gifts for the babies who are born ... We have rattlers for them and recognizing them as our newest community members. And recognizing the moms and parents as well in that. And then we have other gifts for other children, for those who are older ... even though we know they are older, we know that they would love to appreciate gifts. So we made medicine pouches and put sage and juniper in there and gave it to them and ... the kids were just running up wanting one ... And same with the parents, like when we finished with the kids, we gave parents medicine pouches and honoured them for allowing us to be a part of their children's lives for any reason ... We have certificates that we give the parents, honouring them as caregivers and caretakers of their children.

Child protection practice is a complex balancing act in which the practitioner's choices and the family's and community's response interact to influence the nature of intervention. Most practitioners emphasize building trusting relationships, but they differ about whether such relationships should be confined to the nuclear family or incorporate the extended family and the community. Aboriginal and non-Aboriginal practitioners are aware of disempowering, disrespectful, and power-oriented practice. This practice is symbolized by the non-Aboriginal practitioner who is a stranger to the family, who arrives accompanied by police, and who removes a child from the community. When practitioners have relationships of trust with the family and community, the power differential is less, the police are unnecessary, and a practice approach that is supportive, empowering, and inclusive is possible. Such a practice approach is enhanced when a range of support services are available.

10
Social Representations of Child Protection Practice

This chapter synthesizes themes of earlier chapters to create a foundation for an interpretive argument about child protection practice as it relates to Aboriginal children. This argument suggests that the child protection practitioner has distinct needs and that these needs inform different social representations of practice. Social representations are systems of "values, ideas and practices" that enable communication among members of a group by providing them with a "code for social exchange" (Duveen and Lloyd 1993, 91). They reflect the practical everyday knowledge of the ordinary person and provide a means to organize and structure perceptions of social reality (Billig 1993, 43; Moscovici 1984, 17). Social representations are distinct ways of viewing child protection practice with Aboriginal children and families; they inform the day-to-day work of child protection professionals and their communication with each other. I conclude with a discussion of the book's findings in relation to the existing literature as well as with implications for further research, education, policy, and practice.

Synthesis of Themes

Ensuring children's safety is clearly the common foundation to child protection practice, but the ways in which practice is envisioned, the context analyzed, the social condition explained, relevant knowledge described, and practice action outlined vary considerably. Both Aboriginal and non-Aboriginal practitioners at the BC Ministry of Children and Family Development confront a two-dimensional uncertainty in practice. There is uncertainty in the encounter with the child, parents, and family, but there is also uncertainty in the ex post facto response from MCFD management to the decisions the practitioner makes. This uncertainty, intensified by public inquiry, management action, media interest, and the external review of practice, is made more confusing by the complexity of legislative, policy, and organizational changes.

Aboriginal practitioners in Aboriginal organizations face less uncertainty in practice than do non-Aboriginal practitioners as they often begin the investigative process with in-depth knowledge of the family and community, and they often work in organizations described as respectful and supportive. Aboriginal practitioners generally represent the organizational climate positively and often fear the encroachment of the values, policies, and practices of the MCFD. Differentiating their practice from the dominant discourse of the ministry is an ongoing challenge.

Practitioners describe the foundation of child protection intervention as the inability to parent, but they interpret the causes of such inability differently. To some, it is related to poverty, violence, and addictions. To others, it is a consequence of dependency, powerlessness, loss of cultural identity, and colonization. Both Aboriginal and non-Aboriginal practitioners see the parents' residential school experience as being at the heart of today's inability to parent. But it is only Aboriginal practitioners who structure this experience within the interpretative framework of colonization, perhaps because their understanding of this era, and the subsequent child welfare era, is informed by knowledge derived from family and community experience.

Non-Aboriginal practitioners who have had extensive contact with Aboriginal people appear to incorporate different values, strategies, explanations of the social condition, and bases of practice knowledge into their discourse about practice. As awareness of a different world increases, the representation of practice is slowly transformed to resemble that of Aboriginal practitioners in Aboriginal organizations. But the reverse is also true: the representations of Aboriginal practitioners employed at the ministry appear similar to the practice descriptions of other MCFD practitioners. This suggests that the practice context – whether sociopolitical, organizational, cultural, or community – may be the most powerful influence in the creation of practitioners' representations of practice. By contrast, the theoretical, or scientific, basis to practice is much less extensively described, which suggests that scientific knowledge is less influential than is analysis of the social context in the creation of practice representations.

Description of the knowledge and social condition dimensions to practice is marked by the significance of experience. As a foundation to practice, experience appears more influential than scientific facts, theories, or explanations. Whether it is one's family experience of residential school or foster care, one's experience as a parent, or one's practice experience in different communities, experience appears to provide the foundation for theorizing, conceptualizing, and evaluating practice. For example, the experience of growing up in a large family creates openness to the family as a resource for children and generates a practice orientation that searches for family strengths. The experience of living and working in a small community provides the practitioner with a rich network of community relationships and creates a practice orientation that involves community members in planning for a child's safety. The experience of family members attending residential school or being removed by child protection practitioners provides a deep understanding of the exercise of government power and its effects on Aboriginal people. Reflection on these latter experiences generates an orientation to practice that is respectful, non-authoritarian, supportive, and empowering.

Power is exercised in a variety of ways in child protection practice. The most fundamental is the practitioner's power to remove a child from the family, but it also includes the power to remove a child from foster parents or to return a child to the family. Although child protection practitioners exercise these powers, they are, at the same time, objects of the exercise of power. Whether it is the review of practice by a judicial inquiry; the Office of the Children's Commissioner; the Audit and Review Division of the ministry; the Office of the Child, Youth, and Family Advocate; or the media, practitioners experience the effects of power and its exercise in child protection. This experience is most acute when a practitioner or colleague is disciplined. For Aboriginal people, the power inherent in child protection recreates their historic subordination to Canadian society's laws and values. The power inherent in child protection, for MCFD practitioners, reinforces the necessity to conform to the dominant professional culture and leads to cautious, low-risk, rule-oriented practice. Practitioners are aware of the power of their position, but they vary along a continuum with respect to how they exercise that power in practice. Some maximize the power differences between themselves and their clients, whereas others minimize them.

The above discussion suggests that practitioners have three major needs when it comes to child protection practice with Aboriginal children and families: the need to structure uncertainty, to negotiate two worlds, and to create a map of emerging practice. Each is described below.

Structuring Uncertainty

The need to structure uncertainty is most keenly felt by practitioners in the urban offices of the MCFD. Their work is characterized by large caseloads, ongoing encounters with strangers, and a demanding high-volume practice. There is little opportunity to build relationships with clients or to provide ongoing service. The nature of the work is crisis-oriented and short-term. It demands that the practitioner manage the unpredictability of the encounter with clients through personal safety strategies, the ability to think on one's feet, and strategies to enhance credibility in the short term. The practitioner needs to be flexible, adaptable, and calm under pressure. These practitioners, in particular, live with an ongoing level of fear that their practice might, at some unpredictable moment, be cast into the spotlight of external review. This awareness that their practice could at any moment capture management's attention and be subject to disciplinary consequences creates pressure to be cautious, thorough, low-risk, and highly compliant with policy while, at the same time, managing an "outrageous" workload. These multiple demands and conflicting pressures create an ongoing need to structure the uncertainty of daily professional life. This need finds expression in two representations of child protection practice, which I describe below.

Negotiating Two Worlds

The need to negotiate two worlds is most evident in practitioners who are required to cross cultural boundaries in order to practise child protection. Such a practitioner may be an Aboriginal practitioner at the MCFD, a non-Aboriginal practitioner in an Aboriginal organization, or a non-Aboriginal MCFD practitioner working in an Aboriginal community. In each case, everyday professional life is lived by negotiating the differences between the world of an Aboriginal community and the world of a provincial government ministry. As one world is juxtaposed with the other on an ongoing basis, and as the practitioner's understanding of both increases, the limitations, tensions, and contradictions between them become evident. To practise successfully, the practitioner needs to find ways to interpret, advocate, and mediate between these worlds. In short, the practitioner needs to negotiate differences. At times this is possible, but at other times it leads to a sharp awareness of the limitations of existing policy, practice, and service delivery systems.

Creating a Map

The need to create a map of emerging practice is most evident among

Aboriginal practitioners in Aboriginal organizations. Recognizing an absence of cultural autonomy for Aboriginal child welfare due to the imposition of the dominant culture's policies and practices, these practitioners want to conceptualize and describe unique ways of practice. Like the practitioners negotiating two worlds, they are aware that existing policy, practice, and service delivery systems are limited when it comes to meeting the needs of Aboriginal people. But they also see a need to create child welfare policies and practices that blend traditional approaches with the contemporary world. Existing legislation and policy represents the imposition of a foreign system and the continued subjugation of Aboriginal peoples to the dominant society. At the same time, they recognize the unique content of Aboriginal child welfare, and the explication of its values, policies, and practices is a work in progress requiring appropriate language and a map identifying its boundaries, features, and routes. The search for appropriate language and the process of renaming practice to reflect its new meaning is part of creating that map.

The needs described above – to structure uncertainty, to negotiate two worlds, and to create a map of practice – influence the representation of child protection practice. This process is described below.

Social Representations of Child Protection Practice with Aboriginal Children

I believe there are four social representations of child protection practice with Aboriginal children: power-oriented practice, policy-oriented practice, family-oriented practice, and community-oriented practice. Each is described below.

Power-Oriented Practice

Practitioners refer to this representation of practice often enough to suggest its existence, but its full explication remains to be developed. At present, it can be sketched only in a shadowy outline. It is characterized by the overt and ongoing use of power in the practitioner's day-to-day practice with Aboriginal families and communities. In practical terms it is expressed by "barging into houses," using the "power button," developing safety plans and dictating them to parents, demanding compliance without developing a relationship, and threatening the removal of children. In this representation, the practitioner is aware that there is a power difference between Aboriginal families and child protection authorities, and she chooses to establish the maximum differential. Its underlying purpose is to ensure the safety of the child by ensuring parental compliance with the practitioner's expectations. In this representation, the practitioner operates with a good knowledge of legislation and policy requirements but focuses on the safety of the child in relation to the nuclear family. There is little effort directed towards building the credibility of child protection practice, nor is there any emphasis on building a relationship of trust or mutual respect with parents or family members. There is no inclusive vision within which the extended family or community participates in practice decision making. In this representation, the practitioner's need to structure uncertainty is apparent. She lives with an ongoing fear of reprisal from her employer and with an ongoing fear for her personal safety. To manage the unpredictability of the situation, the practitioner uses the power of her position to demand compliance from parents. When such compliance cannot be assured, the practitioner removes the child. For Aboriginal people, the effect of this representation is to reproduce the relations of domination and subordination previously experienced through the Indian Act, the residential schools, and the sixties scoop.

Policy-Oriented Practice

This representation is characterized by the practitioner's emphasis on following the dictates of child protection policy. The practitioner approaches assessment cautiously, with the aim of gathering a complete picture and "leaving no stone unturned." Although employing good crisis intervention and communication skills, and being respectful and supportive of clients, policy-oriented practitioners take few risks in developing an intervention strategy. Overall, their practice is characterized by its rule orientation and high compliance with policy. In the forefront of the practitioner's mind is the question, "What does policy say?" with decision making occurring by considering the child's needs within the context of existing legislation. The practitioner may involve the parents in decision making, but the extended family and community are generally absent. If the child needs to be removed from the family, the practitioner may devote time and energy to ensure that the parent-child relationship is maintained; however, an extensive critique of existing policy or recognition that existing services are inadequate is not part of this practice representation. Generally, there is little evidence of creative interventive planning. The purpose of this practice is to ensure the safety of the child by complying with existing policy guidelines and directives. It does not consider the question: "How might the needs of this child be met in the context of the family's strengths and the community's resources?" This representation is found principally among practitioners at the BC Ministry of Children and Family Development and is likely the dominant form of practice in the province. Like power-oriented practice, it is influenced by the practitioner's need to structure uncertainty and to reduce fear. It aims to avoid anger and abuse from clients through implementing effective intervention strategies. It avoids reprisal from the employer through complying with policy. Its aim is to ensure the safety not only of the child but also of the practitioner.

Family-Oriented Practice
This practice representation sees the strengths of the extended family as a resource for ensuring the safety and well-being of the child. It may be informed by the practitioner's own experience of life in a large family (Aboriginal or non-Aboriginal) or by observations made while working with Aboriginal families. It may also have developed through an introduction to family systems theory while acquiring a university education in social work. In this representation the child is placed at the centre of the extended family, and her/his needs are considered in relation to the resources of the family. The practitioner searches for a family's strengths. Her communication skills are used to develop a trusting relationship with the family and to build credibility for an intervention that incorporates family resources. Although the practitioner is aware of the general requirements of legislation and policy, these do not occupy centre stage. If the resources of the extended family cannot meet the needs of the child, then alternate caregivers are incorporated in order to ensure her/his safety and well-being; however, the practitioner recognizes that the family continues to exist in the child's mind even if the two are separated. This representation is found among Aboriginal and non-Aboriginal practitioners as well as within Aboriginal organizations and the MCFD. It appears more frequently among practitioners in reserve communities and small towns, where the practitioner and family members have an ongoing relationship characterized by credibility and trust.

Community-Oriented Practice
This practice representation begins with the assumption that communities have a responsibility to protect children and should intervene to ensure their safety and well-being. It functions as an extension of the family-oriented representation but incorporates the community into the work of child protection. The child is at the centre of a social net-

work that begins with the nuclear family, moves outward to the extended family, and then incorporates the community. There is an acknowledged interdependence between the child, the family, and the community. Intervention with respect to a child has a ripple effect that extends outwards and intervention with respect to the community has an acknowledged beneficial effect on the child. Community and family resources are made available to meet the needs of the child. Whenever possible, the community is incorporated into child protection intervention – whether it is risk assessment, safety planning, resource development, alternative care provision, or prevention. The precise boundary between family and community can be unclear, but for child protection intervention it includes band council members, resource personnel (band social development worker, alcohol and drug counsellor, youth worker), teachers, elders, and extended family members. At its heart, this representation has a vision of practice that is community-inclusive and that searches for ways to incorporate the community at various interventive stages. While this representation is most common among Aboriginal practitioners in Aboriginal communities, it can also be found among some MCFD practitioners, particularly those in small towns or isolated reserve communities. This representation demands that the non-Aboriginal practitioner negotiate between the world of the Aboriginal community and the world of MCFD child protection policy and practice. It informs the map-making process for the Aboriginal practitioner. At its fullest expression, the community reclaims its historic obligation to protect children, and the government has no role in this.

Relationship of Findings to the Existing Literature
The findings reported in *Protecting Aboriginal Children* suggest that the dichotomy between child-centred and family-centred child welfare may be an oversimplification. In the existing child welfare literature there is a tendency to juxtapose the child with the family when describing child welfare intervention (Parton 1997; Nelson 1984; Weisman 1994). The Gove Inquiry in British Columbia is no exception to this trend, arguing that one of the "sources of failure" in the province's child welfare system was the move from a child-centred to a family-centred system in 1993. It proposed a return to a child-centred system within the framework of a multidisciplinary team (Gove 1995, 2:89). Although practitioners agree that ensuring the well-being of the child is central to their practice, they differ significantly concerning how to accomplish this goal. The four representations of practice described above suggest that

power, policy, family, and community are significant themes in the representation of child protection practice. The dichotomy of child-centred versus family-centred practice leaves out significant dimensions of child protection practice, especially with regard to Aboriginal children.

Child protection practice is stressful, complex, has personal safety risks, requires the ability to think on one's feet, and does not provide immediate recognition of one's efforts. This echoes themes from Callahan's child protection practice research in British Columbia. She found child protection practice "complex, fast-paced, risky, solitary, invisible, and contradictory" (Callahan 1993, 73). These themes would be supported by many practitioners who are employed at the MCFD. However, Aboriginal practitioners in Aboriginal organizations suggest that knowledge of the extended family and community changes the nature of their practice. Risks to personal safety are reduced, the pace of work is different, the practitioner and the practice are visible within the community, and practice has an inclusive rather than a non-inclusive character. In this respect, the findings of *Protecting Aboriginal Children* provide a more comprehensive understanding of child protection practice in British Columbia than is presently available because Callahan's study focused on non-Aboriginal women. Although Callahan (1993) referred to the contradictory roles of the child protection practitioner within the family, she did not identify contradictions that are rooted in the policies and system of child protection.

The practitioners I interviewed described the stressful nature of child protection practice – a finding supported by a study of child welfare practitioners in the United States. They have been found to have higher job stress levels and less job satisfaction than have other social work practitioners (Wares and Dobrec 1992). By contrast, a national survey of Indian Child Welfare program administrators in the United States found that only 3 percent were partially or totally dissatisfied with their jobs (ibid.). While these data assess child protection practice in a different national context and compare administrators in Aboriginal organizations with practitioners in non-Aboriginal organizations, the general theme of the findings corresponds to the differences I found between practitioners' descriptions of the organizational climate in the MCFD and that in Aboriginal organizations.

The annual reports of the Office of the Child, Youth, and Family Advocate and the Office of the Children's Commissioner echo the absence of prevention programs and adequate support services described by practitioners. The Advocate's Office "is most concerned about inadequate early intervention services and funding, inadequate services to older youth and seriously inadequate services for children in government care." (Office of the Child, Youth, and Family Advocate 1999). The Office of the Children's Commissioner observes that "the importance of prevention and early support and intervention is a persistent theme in all of our findings," and notes that the ministry has not yet addressed province-wide implementation of an early intervention program (Pallan 2000). Practitioners make reference to their absence, particularly in small rural and reserve communities.

A distinguishing feature of some child protection practice in Aboriginal communities is a participatory approach that includes the extended family in decision making. I have documented and described more variations on family-inclusive decision making in the protection of Aboriginal children than are found in British Columbia by Herbert (1995b) or in Newfoundland by Pennell and Burford (1997) in the Family Group Decision Making Project. I have also described how the community is included in child protection decision making. The community's significance to Aboriginal peoples in their approach to child welfare has been identified in the literature, but *Protecting Aboriginal Children* expands on this theme. Existing literature suggests that "the care and education of the young is a responsibility shared not just by parents, but by the extended family and the entire community. In these settings, no child is ever lost or alone" (Boyer 1992, 25). Sometimes the extended family is described in a way that suggests it is synonymous with the community when it comes to the protection of children (McKenzie, Seidl, and Bone 1995). In addition, the importance of community control of services for Aboriginal peoples has been stressed (Armitage 1993a; Wharf 1991), and the different characteristics of communities in which child protection takes place have been noted (MacDonald 1997). However, the distinctive ways in which communities and practitioners interact and/or represent the nature of their relationship with regard to the protection of Aboriginal children has not previously been identified.

This book echoes previously identified themes about the significance of the residential school era to the parenting inability of today's Aboriginal parents (Ing 1991; RCAP 1996, 3). However, placing the inability to parent within the context of colonization theories is not echoed in the literature on Aboriginal people, the residential schools, or colonization. Some describe the residential schools as a form of genocide (Chrisjohn, Young, and Maraun 1997), while others refer to the child protection system as a form of cultural genocide (Community Panel 1992), and others interpret Aboriginal peoples' experience in Canada as colonization (Adams 1999; Hudson 1997; McKenzie and Hudson 1985;

Morrissette, McKenzie, and Morrissette 1993). D'Souza (1994) argues that Australian Aboriginal child welfare policy contains unrecognized elements of colonization. However, the literature tends towards analyzing government or child welfare policy as colonization rather than viewing the inability to parent as the effect of colonization.

I have argued throughout this book that different visions of practice lead to different outcomes. Some Aboriginal and non-Aboriginal practitioners place considerable emphasis on the extended family and community in child protection practice. Others do not incorporate cultural difference as a factor in practice decision making and appear to practice in a "culture-neutral" way. This approach, summarized by the phrase "I treat them no different than anyone else" suggests that practice may be power- or policy-oriented but not family- or community-oriented. Failure to recognize the significance of the extended family and community in child protection practice with Aboriginal children is cited by Zylberberg (1991) as "the greatest failing of the child protection system." He argues that "many social workers, ignorant of Indian cultural values and social norms, make decisions that are wholly inappropriate in the context of Indian family life and so they frequently discover neglect or abandonment where none exists" (77). This finding is confirmed by a study of culturally selective perception in child protection decision making (Dumont 1988). It compared the practice of two Aboriginal social workers who have bachelor of social work degrees (BSWs) with one Caucasian social worker who has a master of social work degree (MSW). Fifty-one percent of the caseload of the MSW practitioner was in government care compared to 21 percent and 28 percent, respectively, of the caseloads of the Aboriginal practitioners. The sample size in this study is very small, and the difference may be due to other factors. But it does suggest that cultural perception is a factor in the way practitioners make assessments and decisions about removing children. Nelson, Kelley, and McPherson (1985) assert that there are different ways of helping in an Aboriginal community. An Aboriginal community is a network with a high number of complex interrelationships. Members of the community play multiple roles in relation to one another – friend, neighbour, relative, and community service volunteer – and the child or family that is the focus of concern is embedded within this community network. This relationship reinforces my findings about the significance of community and culture to practice, but it misses the significance of organizational context and extensive contact with Aboriginal people to thinking about practice.

My findings support earlier work that demonstrates that neither theoretically guided practice nor the use of social work theory in child protection practice is anything but minimal. In the social work academy strong arguments can be found concerning the value of a theoretically informed social work practice (Bartlett 1970; Payne 1997; Carew 1979). In spite of strong exhortations by social work educators and considerable teaching emphasis in schools of social work, there is little evidence that social work theory guides social work practice. As early as 1931 Karpf found little evidence "that the caseworker used any other than the common sense concepts and judgments relating to the attitudes, emotional states, personality and personality traits of the client" (Carew 1979, 349). Carew, in an exploratory study of twenty British social workers in 1979, found that the use of theoretical knowledge as a basis for activities in practice "was minimal." Some evidence suggests that social work students are able to integrate theory with practice (Barsky, Rogers, Krysik, and Langevin 1997) and that new graduates are able to retain their personal models of practice early in their careers (Payne 1997, 52). However, my research provides little evidence that scientific knowledge guides child protection practice when practitioners have been practising for more than two years.

Implications for Social Work Research and Education
Largely absent from the published literature on Aboriginal child welfare is any systematic analysis of the effects of the removal of Aboriginal children from their families and communities and their placement in non-Aboriginal homes as either foster children or adoptees. In comparison with the residential school era, the child welfare era, which began in the mid-1950s and continues today, is relatively unstudied. At present, statistics, memories, and arguments constitute the literature in this area. There are statistics on the percentage of Aboriginal children who have been adopted or who are in government care. There are also memories of child welfare intervention during the sixties scoop (Fournier and Crey 1997). In addition, there are observations and arguments about the loss of cultural identity occurring to Aboriginal people due to their placement in foster care. However, no research that assesses the effects on Aboriginal children of long-term foster care or adoption is available.

Similarly, literature that documents and describes Aboriginal child-rearing practices and their variations between Aboriginal communities is unavailable. Although the negative impact of the residential school on child-rearing is well known, the description of positive child-rearing practices has not been studied. *Protecting Aboriginal Children* documents extended family and community involvement in the care and protection of children. However, more systematic inquiry into how extended families and communities carry out their responsibilities to care and protect children is needed. What variations are found across Aboriginal communities? Are there limitations to extended family and community involvement as a strategy to protect children? Are such methods transferable beyond reserve communities and rural areas to urban communities and metropolitan areas?

I have conceptualized five dimensions to child protection practice and have explored each. From this analysis, context appeared to strongly influence practice action, whereas scientific knowledge did not. However, the relationship between context and values (or theory and experience or explanation and action) is unstudied. In short, little is known about the relative significance of the various dimensions of child protection practice to practice action. In addition, within some dimensions little is known about the relative significance of the various factors identified. For example, I have identified a range of factors within the social condition, such as poverty, alcoholism, violence, the residential schools, and loss of identity. To determine how practitioners organize their thinking in relation to these factors requires further investigation.

Some non-Aboriginal practitioners recognize that there are cultural differences between themselves and Aboriginal people, but others do not. This suggests the existence of culturally blind child protection practice. Some schools of social work in British Columbia prepare students to work with Aboriginal communities by having them take a required course in First Nations issues. Although such a course introduces practitioners to the ideas, values, and history informing Aboriginal culture, it oversimplifies the task of developing an ability to understand difference, bridge cultures, and negotiate cultural worlds. Today, social work students enter a multicultural practice world that demands they have the ability to understand and recognize difference. Further study of research findings and educational strategies, as well as program evaluation knowledge, is required if we are to expect competent practice with different populations.

The foundation to social work's claim to professional status rests on the belief that its practice has a scientific foundation. However, I have demonstrated that child protection practitioners with a social work education make little use of scientific knowledge in practice; rather, experience – whether professional, personal, familial, or communal – appears most influential in practice decision making. Although experience is arguably a powerful influence in life, little is known about how it intersects with ideas, theories, or facts in the course of a social work education. Today's educators provide considerable opportunity to reflect on experience – whether through participating in classroom exercises or writing assignments – but the relationship such reflection has to the conceptualization of practice is not known. Similarly, the intersection between reflection on experience and social work practice theory needs to be explored in order to determine effective ways of integrating experience, theory, and practice.

Implications for Policy and Practice
I found that child protection practitioners with lower caseloads, fewer paperwork requirements, and support for practice from management and fellow practitioners tend towards providing social representations of practice that are family- or community-oriented. These social representations are respectful and inclusive, minimize the power differential, emphasize relationship building, and recognize family and community strengths. Creativity, dialogue, and innovative solutions to problems require an interpersonal and organizational climate that fosters this kind of practice. Organizational leaders can take significant steps to create such a climate. However, such organizational conditions require resources not simply in order to reduce the caseload size and paperwork requirements but also to provide practitioners with a range of options for practice decision making. The harm to Aboriginal children, families, and communities brought on by child removal is well documented; but the alternative requires resources for family and community supports that are largely absent in British Columbia – particularly in isolated rural communities. To encourage family- and community-oriented social representations of practice – representations that would seem to be congruent with Aboriginal culture, values, and aspirations – we need more support resources. Whether these resources are used to free a child protection practitioner to develop alternate care resources, to provide additional family support, or to implement an early intervention or prevention strategy, they are an essential complement to practice decision making in a time of crisis.

Protecting Aboriginal Children provides contrasting representations of the organizational context of practice. The BC Ministry of Children and Family Development, a large centralized bureaucracy with many management levels, emanates a climate of fear and reprisal and is viewed as unsupportive of practitioners. Aboriginal organizations are small, local, often have only one management level, and are generally viewed as respectful and supportive of practitioners. While one organization has a universal focus and serves the dominant culture, the other has a specific focus and serves only Aboriginal families. In spite of these distinctions, the difference in organizational climate suggests that practitioners in Aboriginal organizations have more support to develop and use their knowledge of the community in practice, to invite the community to engage in child protection practice, and to participate in the community. In fact, these practitioners frequently cite the value and significance of the community to child protection practice. A decentralized model of service delivery is able to recognize and value community interaction in child protection practice with Aboriginal communities. This model creates opportunities for increased community interaction and easy access to decision makers. It also encourages participation on the part of extended families and communities.

The recent creation of Aboriginal child welfare organizations places demands on the state to recognize "difference" in child welfare policy and practice. Aboriginal organizations and their representatives assert that the needs of the Aboriginal community for child protection are different than the needs of the dominant society, and the fulfillment of those needs demands different policies, practices, and funding formulae. At issue here is the tension between the universal rules and standards of a provincial child welfare system and the needs of a cultural community to develop policies and practices that ensure the well-being of its children in culturally appropriate ways. As the number of Aboriginal child welfare organizations increases and other cultural communities demand to have their needs recognized, the pressure to accommodate difference will intensify. This will create a challenging policy climate within which to maintain the universal objectives of child welfare policy while recognizing difference in legislation, policy, and practice.

Appendix 1:
Note on the Theoretical Framework

The study of child protection can be approached from several vantage points, such as policy analysis, historical development, problematic cases, clients' perspectives, and women's experience. This study explores social workers' descriptions and explanations of their practice because this area of study has been neglected. Child protection practice involves direct interaction with children and families to ensure children's safety and well-being, but it is also embedded within legal, bureaucratic, and social relationships. To capture this complexity, I needed a theoretical perspective permitting analysis of thought about direct intervention with children as well as the social context of practice. In addition, the theoretical perspective must enable the identification and integration of the major ideas orienting practice in order to enable us to understand the thinking that structures action.

I chose the perspective of social representations because it is a flexible theoretical framework, it enables thought about action to be organized and analyzed in an integrated way, it permits analysis of the social context of practice, and it captures symbolic forms of thought. Social representations are a "system of values, ideas, and practices that establish a consensual order among phenomena" and "enable communication to take place among the members of a community by providing them with a code for social exchange" (Moscovici in Duveen and Lloyd 1993, 91).

The perspective of social representations provides a range of opportunities to better understand child protection practice. First, social representations function to capture social workers' holistic thinking about practice. This enables the interrelationships between value, culture, theory, scientific knowledge, opinion, and action to be explored in a practice context. Second, the social representations perspective enables reflection on the social context of practice. It recognizes the child protection social worker as a thinking person whose practice is embedded in the institutional, bureaucratic, and cultural relationships of society. Third, social representations capture symbolic forms of thinking about practice. Symbolic thinking powerfully shapes perception and orients behaviour. Fourth, social representations encourage exploration of the worldview of practitioners. By identifying common ideas among practitioners, the social identity of the child protection social worker can be better understood. In short, the perspective of social representations is holistic and encourages the exploration of the "mental mind set" that lies behind behaviour, attitude, opinion, and value. It aims to identify the central ideas and the relationships between ideas that structure, orient, and justify social practice.

Origins

The origin of the concept of social representations can be found in the work of Emile Durkheim (Deutscher 1984, 76). Durkheim emphasized the significance of collective representations to distinguish them from individual representations in social life (Verguerre 1989, 10). Durkheim argued that an individual representation is a purely psychic phenomenon that is not reducible to cerebral activity. A collective representation, similarly, cannot be reduced to the individuals that comprise society because it affirms the primacy of the social over the individual (Herzlich 1981, 303). To Durkheim, representations "act as stabilizers for many words or ideas" and include a whole range of intellectual forms – science, religion, myth, as well as modalities of time and space, ideas, emotions, and beliefs (Farr and Moscovici 1984, 17, 19). Moscovici (1976) argued that this definition was too broad and proposed to define social representations as

> an intermediate stage between concept and perception based in the dimensions of attitude, information, and images contributing to the development of behavior and social communication leading to the processes of objectification, classification and anchoring characterized by a focus on a social relation and a pressure towards inference, and above all elaborated in different modalities of communication: broadcasting, propagation, and propaganda.

La psychanalyse: Son image et son public, his book about the common sense understanding of psychoanalytic theory in France, was published in 1961. It marked the beginning of contemporary interest in social representations. Since that time, social representations theory has been used to study subjects such as health, mental illness, social gender, breastfeeding, conception, the child, urban space, schooling, justice, and professional practice. Scholarly interest in social representations is confined primarily to European social psychology and is concentrated among researchers in France, Switzerland, and Italy (Emler and Ohana 1993; Zani 1993). A few researchers in England (Farr 1993; Breakwell and Canter 1993) and Quebec (Bertrand 1993) are concerned with the study of social representations. At the same time, social representations are also a subject of multidisciplinary interest. Anthropologists, historians, philosophers, and sociologists have all incorporated the idea of social representations into their work. The perspective of social representations has been employed to study professional practice in psychology (Palmonari and Pombeni 1984), nursing, and psychiatric nursing (Zani 1993; 1987).

Major Themes

Central to the perspective of social representations is the belief that psychological states are socially produced and that our representations determine our reactions. Representations are not "individually produced replicas of perceptual data" but social creations, and they are, therefore, a part of social reality (Billig 1993, 43). A second theme is that social representations reflect a common sense understanding of the social world. As Moscovici notes, social representations are formulated through action and communication in society and are "a specific way of understanding and communicating what we know already" (Farr and Moscovici 1984, 17). They reflect the practical everyday knowledge of the ordinary person rather than expert or scientific knowledge. A third theme is that social representations organize and structure our perception of social reality. A representation is the "product of processes of mental activity through which an individual or group reconstitutes the reality with which it is confronted and to which it attributes a specific meaning" (Abric 1994, 13). However, it is more than just a reflection of that reality. It also provides a "meaningful organization" of reality and functions as a "system of interpretation" that governs relationships between individuals and their physical and social environment. As representations determine both behaviour and practice, they thereby act as "guides for action" (ibid.).

The social representations perspective recognizes human beings as "thinking persons," capable of asking questions, seeking answers, and, in general, thinking about life (Farr and Moscovici 1984). Interest in social representations derives from studying the social nature of thinking and the importance of thinking in human life (Billig 1993, 40). It also acknowledges a historical dimension to ideas in social life. In other words, social representations are part of a society's collective memory and are the "substratum of images and meanings without which no collectivity can operate" (Farr and Moscovici 1984, 19). Although they are linked to previous systems, images, and schema, they should not be viewed as permanent or static. They are: "social entities with a life of their own communicating between themselves, opposing each other and changing in harmony with the course of life, vanishing only to re-emerge in new guises" (Moscovici 1984, 10).

Functions
Moscovici (1984, 24) argues that the purpose of social representations is "to make the unfamiliar familiar," and Doise (1986, 84) argues that it is "to regulate relations between social actors." Within these general purposes, four functions of social representations can be identified: (1) the knowledge function, (2) the identity function, (3) the guidance function, and (4) the justificatory function (Abric 1994, 15-18). The knowledge function enables reality to be understood and explained. Social representations permit social actors to acquire, integrate, and assimilate knowledge in a coherent fashion in relation to their cognitive system and values. This permits the communication, exchange, and diffusion of "common sense" knowledge about the world. The identity function situates individuals and groups in a social field and enables the development of a social identity compatible with the norms and values of the society. Social representations play a role in identity construction through a process involving the social comparison between groups – distinguishing one group from another. These also exert an influence on the social control and socialization of group members. The orientation function guides behaviour and practice in three ways. First, the representation intervenes directly in the "définition de la finalité de la situation." That is, it defines a priori the relevant relations for the subject and also the cognitive steps to be taken. Second, the representation selects and filters information in order to make the subject's interpretation of reality conform to it. In this sense, the representation precedes and determines the interaction. Third, the representation is prescriptive. It is reflective of the rules and social relationships of the society, and it defines what behaviour will or will not be tolerated in a given society. The justificatory function permits after-the-fact justification of "les prises de position" (position taking) and behaviour. Representations also provide justifications for social differences between groups – particularly when stereotypes and hostility are evident.

Processes

Social representations are generated through two processes: anchoring and objectification. Anchoring strives to reduce strange ideas to ordinary categories and images and to set them in a familiar context. Objectification turns an abstract idea into something almost concrete and thereby transfers something in the mind's eye to something existing in the physical world (Moscovici 1984, 29).

Anchoring "draws something foreign and disturbing that intrigues us into our particular system of categories and compares it to the paradigm of a category which we think to be suitable" (Moscovici 1984, 29). Fundamental to anchoring is the process of classification and naming: "By classifying what is unclassifiable and naming what is unnamable, we are able to imagine it, to represent it ... And by so doing we reveal our 'theory' of society and of human nature" (Moscovici 1984, 30).

Objectification is the process by which mental content is turned into reality (Wagner, Elejabarrieta, and Lahnsteiner 1995, 672). It consists of identifying or constructing an iconic aspect for a new or difficult-to-grasp concept, theory, or idea (ibid.). As Moscovici (1984, 38) notes, to objectify is "to discover the iconic quality of an imprecise idea or being, to reproduce a concept in an image." Through this process, a figurative nucleus, or a complex of images that captures the essence of the concept, theory, or idea, is identified. This figurative nucleus has an image structure "that visibly reproduces a complex of ideas" (ibid.). During this process ideas are taken literally and attributed with physical reality. They are detached from their social sources and turned into empirical phenomena confirmed by the senses (Wagner, Elejabarrieta, and Lahnsteiner 1995, 672).

Metaphors, like images, are an important device in the objectification process as they make something less familiar more familiar (Wagner, Elejabarrieta, and Lahnsteiner 1995, 674). Metaphors also provide a basic structure for stories about problematic situations in the social services. Practitioners set problems through metaphors and orient action towards resolution through the stories they tell about problematic situations. The stories, encapsulated by metaphors, provide a structure for problem-setting and problem-solving (Schon 1993, 143). Although metaphors can be observed in many social representations, not all metaphors are instances of objectification.

Objectification has a dependent relationship to the characteristics of the social group in which the representation is formed. "The specific social conditions of a certain group favour specific kinds of images, metaphors, or symbols to be used as objectification 'devices' i.e. 'tools'

by which the end of understanding through objectification is achieved"
(Wagner, Elejabarrieta, and Lahnsteiner 1995, 673). "A new idea only
diffuses in a group if an image, metaphor or symbol is found and used
in public discourse which (a) appeals to a qualified majority of the target population and (b) captures the essentials of the new idea" (674). It
need not be true, correct, or accurate: it need only be "good to think
with."

Professional practice creates a unique set of challenges for the perspective of social representations. The nature of a profession implies the
application of scientific or expert knowledge to the resolution of human problems. However, this does not negate the potential for creative
problem-solving arising from a common sense understanding of the
world. In professional practice a tension exists between the problems
arising from everyday life that are presented to the practitioner and the
availability of scientific knowledge to resolve those problems. In deciding on a course of action to resolve a problem, the professional may
blend scientific knowledge, professional theory, common sense explanation, personal belief, and professional values. The result is a unique
individual set of ideas that inform, orient, and justify practice. These
ideas may, to some extent, be socially shared among professionals in
the same field of practice.

Field of the Representation
The exploration of social representations in relation to social practice is
potentially limitless, but it can be circumscribed theoretically by introducing the concept of the field of the representation. However, the idea
of field is complex. It expresses: "The idea of an organization of the
content: there is a representational field where there is hierarchical unity
of the elements, but also the relative richness of this content as well as
the qualitative and imaging properties of the representation. In this
sense, the representational field presupposes a minimum of information that it integrates in images and in return assists in organizing"
(Herzlich 1981, 310).

However, Bourdieu argues that the idea of field can also convey: "A
group of social objects having between them hierarchical and
oppositional relations that structure precisely the distribution between
these objects of a specific capital having social value" (Doise 1986, 85).

This perspective argues that social relationships within a field will
mirror class relationships in the field of productive relations. Actors in a
field either know or accept the distribution of a field's values and can
deny their relationship to other interests in the field. Individual partici-

pation in a field is guided by two ideas: "habitus" and "disposition." Disposition suggests a system of ordering or classification, a mental structure, a symbolic form, or a historical schema of perception that is the product of class divisions and that incorporates the fundamental structures of the society. Bourdieu argues that these structures produce "les habitus," long-lasting social arrangements that structure social practice (Doise 1986, 88). This interpretation suggests that social representations in a field will have a certain regularity and durability and will be informed or shaped by the social divisions of the society.

Field of Child Welfare Practice

To permit child protection practice to be more clearly identified and its significant dimensions conceptualized, I introduce the concept of field of practice. The idea of field also serves as an informal conceptual linkage between practice and its representation.

Child welfare is one field of social work practice. A field of practice in social work refers to: "the distinctive settings, population groups, or social problem areas in which social workers practice and to which social workers adapt their practice" (Kamerman 1998, 291). The concept of a field of practice assumes that "there is a core foundation of social work knowledge, values, and skills that applies to all social work practice but that the arena in which social workers practice is so large and diversified that there are distinctive variations in practice" (297).

Fields are viewed as more fluid than social work methods because "they emerge, disappear, combine, and recombine in response to social change, new social problems, changing values, and new legislation" (Kamerman 1998, 309). Interest in fields of practice has been found in US social work since the 1920s and re-emerged in the 1960s with the explosion of the personal social services and the interest of the Council on Social Work Education. Bartlett argued that fields of practice are a "characteristic feature of social work" (Bartlett 1965, 758) and that a "stable constellation of organized services, theory, methods, and other characteristics" should be recognized as fields (Kamerman 1998, 295). Although child welfare has been recognized as a field since the 1920s, it is not clear what constitutes the dimensions of a field. Two frameworks are available to assess potential practice fields, suggesting possible dimensions for the field of child welfare practice (Kamerman 1998; Bartlett 1965). Fundamentally, Bartlett argues, a field of practice requires a "human need or social problem" (Kamerman 1998, 296), whereas Kamerman argues it must have a "target or focal point" that describes "the distinctive settings, population groups or social problem areas in which social workers practice" (291). It also requires "organized services" (Bartlett in Kamerman 1998, 296) or "program models and a delivery system" (Kamerman 1998, 306). Bartlett argues there must be "a distinctive social work contribution to the overall program or population" (Kamerman 1998, 296), and Kamerman believes there must be evidence of "earlier historical responses" (302). To Bartlett, there must be a demonstration of "the common and essential elements of all social work practice – knowledge, values, and intervention techniques" (Kamerman 1998, 296). Identifiable "modes of practice (interventions) and staffing patterns" are also required (Kamerman 1998, 307). A field of practice also consists of specialized competence (Bartlett in Kamerman 1998, 296), relevant legislation and policy (Kamerman 1998, 304), research and evaluation outcomes (308), and issues, trends, and debates (309).

These two frameworks, designed to assess potential practice fields, can be analyzed and their content synthesized to suggest dimensions for the field of child welfare practice. The *social condition dimension* provides a description of the needs, issues, problems, and conditions to which intervention is addressed. It includes analysis and explanation of the condition, and incorporates a precise description of the populations and groups to be served. The *contextual dimension* recognizes that child protection practice takes place within a framework of organized social relationships. Social workers and their clients meet and interact within a framework sanctioned by society and structured by a legislative mandate, a bureaucratic organization, and the social provision of helping resources. Implicit within the contextual dimension of practice is a set of power relationships that structure the social worker's relationship to the client and the social worker's relationship to the wider society through the authority of the state. "The institutional alignments – the politics – that form the context of social work practice change in each generation and in so changing periodically reconstitute the practice" (Rein and White 1981, 3).

The *knowledge dimension* to child protection practice refers to the theory, concepts, generalizations, and research used to inform practice. It recognizes that social work action should be under the conscious guidance of knowledge (Bartlett 1961, 25). Although knowledge is recognized as a basic component to social work practice, the relationship of knowledge to practice is unclear (Roberts 1990; Carew 1979). Social work knowledge has tended to be based in the knowledge of other disciplines and professions. Child protection practice may be consistent with this trend and rely extensively on medical and legal knowledge to inform practice.

The *normative dimension* fundamentally recognizes social work practice as a normative activity informed by philosophy, purpose, attitude, value, and ideals (Roberts 1990, 23). These provide a framework for the interpretation of need, the explanation of conditions, and the arguments made to justify intervention. The purpose need not be envisioned as a "grand and shared purpose" and the philosophy need not be viewed as logically consistent (Rein and White 1981, 5). It can be composed of a less than coherent set of images, metaphors, anecdotes, and stories that relate meaning to action. This normative content provides, on the one hand, the locus of consensual values as well as the clues to difference in purpose and philosophy.

The *action dimension* recognizes the methods, skills, and techniques required by the child protection practitioner to respond to needs. It also refers to the helping process – the conscious and systematic ways of acting and interacting with others to encourage change. This involves observation, assessment, action planning, intervention, and evaluation (Barlett 1961). These actions comprise the major steps of "doing" child protection practice.

I have used the social representations perspective to analyze child protection practice. More specifically, I have explored the social representations found in the field of child welfare by focusing on child protection practice as it relates to Aboriginal children. The concept of a representational field suggests that there will be a level of organization, structure, and regularity to the representations of practice. Interview data are analyzed within five dimensions: the social condition dimension, the contextual dimension, the knowledge dimension, the normative dimension, and the action dimension. My methodology is described in Appendix 2.

Appendix 2:
Note on Methodology

Data Collection Method

The purpose of *Protecting Aboriginal Children* is to describe child protection practice and to identify social representations that structure, orient, and justify that practice. Since social representations operate freely in society, are historical phenomena, and are integral to culture, unstructured qualitative methods are most appropriate (Farr 1993, 23, 29, 33). The method of choice associated with this form of naturalistic inquiry is the non-directive interview (Lipiansky 1991, 44). Herzlich argues that the conversational interview is the only method appropriate to the study of social representations (Farr 1993, 30). Sometimes social representations are effectively identified only through argument and oppositions (Billig 1993, 46). In such cases, the conversational interview is an effective medium through which to present arguments and to explore their opposition. However, social representations of child protection practice initially require "thick descriptions" of practice from "encultured informants." Methods that do not prejudge responses or limit the reflexive potential of study participants to explore their life world are key. Since child protection practitioners are embedded in organizational, cultural, and political contexts that constrain liberty of expression (e.g., the public servant role), it is important to create conditions of safety and security for study participants. A sense of confidence in the researcher and trust in the research process are essential to effective reflection.

I represent a different culture, gender, and class than that represented by many of my study participants. An interview process that is engaged and dialogical rather than detached and objectivist is necessary in order to minimize the potential for misunderstanding based on social differences. It is also necessary in order to maximize opportunities for participants to openly reflect about practice and to explore complex interconnections in their reality as child protection practitioners. I chose the conversational interview because it encourages the expression of subjective reality – participants' feelings, self-understandings, and explanations of action.

I used an interview guide with a series of open-ended questions designed to explore the five dimensions of child protection practice identified in the theoretical framework: the social condition dimension, the normative dimension, the contextual dimension, the knowledge dimension, and the action dimension. I asked a series of questions within each dimension, although not necessarily in the order provided in the guide. Additional questions were asked where necessary to seek clarification or to explore a response in greater depth. The interview took the form of a focused conversation, also known as a semi-structured interview (Rubin and Rubin 1995, 5).

Most interviews took place at participants' work sites during normal work hours (e.g., 8:30 AM to 4:30 PM Monday to Friday). Two telephone interviews were conducted with study participants in distant locations. Each interview took between one and one-half hours and two hours.

Selection of Study Participants

Study participants are child protection social workers who were selected from the two major providers of child welfare services to Aboriginal children in British Columbia – the BC Ministry of Children and Family Development and Aboriginal child welfare organizations. A child protection worker is someone who has the authority to remove a child from the care of the family and to place her/him in government care. The basic criteria used to select participants were:

1. The participant has a bachelor of social work or master of social work degree.
2. The participant is either a direct service child protection practitioner or is the direct supervisor of child protection practitioners.
3. The participant is employed by: (a) the BC Ministry for Children and Family Development or (b) an Aboriginal child welfare organization in British Columbia.
4. The participant is responsible for investigating child abuse and neglect and making decisions regarding the removal of a child from the family (i.e., she has protection authority).
5. The participant has had a minimum of two years full-time experience in child protection social work practice since the completion of a bachelor of social work degree.

In addition to these basic criteria, study participants fulfilled the following criteria:

- a great number were female social workers (e.g., 70 percent to 80 percent women) so as to reflect the gender balance of the profession and
child welfare practice;
- some practised in a cross-cultural setting (e.g., an Aboriginal social
worker employed by the Ministry of Children and Family Development or a non-Aboriginal social worker employed by an Aboriginal
child welfare organization);
- some were front-line supervisors;
- some were in rural generalist offices. That is, they had responsibility
for children in care, family service, and adoption in addition to child
protection practice;
- some were in specialized child protection offices;
- some were employed within each of the three models of Aboriginal
child welfare organization in British Columbia (e.g., band bylaw, tripartite agreement, delegated authority).

I conducted interviews with 19 participants: 15 women and 4 men, 12
non-Aboriginal and 7 Aboriginal, 15 with BSW degrees and 3 with MSW
degrees, 1 with other education, 13 front-line child protection practitioners, 6 first-level supervisors, 12 employed by the BC Ministry of Children
and Family Development, and 7 employed by Aboriginal organizations.
Nine MCFD offices and four Aboriginal organizations are represented. I
could not find an Aboriginal male social worker with a BSW/MSW education and two years' child protection practice experience.

Process of Data Collection

To understand fully the complexity of social workers' thinking about
their child protection practice, I needed a wide range of practice perspectives. This research phenomenon, thought of as a "theater in the
round," required me to select as many vantage points about "centre
stage" as possible (Rubin and Rubin 1995, 69). Initially, culture, gender,
organizational auspices, practice organization (e.g., generalist versus
specialist) and cross-cultural practice were assumed to provide the entry
to different vantage points in practice perspective. However, study participants were also located in several regions of the province. Initially,
participants were selected through my contacts with child protection
practitioners in British Columbia. Additional participants were suggested
through the research process. From time to time I explored my profes-

sional network to identify practitioners who met specific criteria (e.g., male social workers with extensive contact with Aboriginal children). I also travelled to six sites in British Columbia to conduct interviews. Access to additional sites was possible through telephone interviews. In addition, some participants had practised in more than one location, which gave access to additional sites. Differences were explored until little new data was being produced and a saturation point appeared to have been reached (Glaser and Strauss 1967). This became clear with the frequent repetition of MCFD participants' concerns about workload, stress, paperwork, and fear of management reprisal for errors. It became apparent with Aboriginal participants' frequent discussion of the significance of the extended family and community and the respectful atmosphere for practice found within Aboriginal organizations. This point of saturation occurred after nineteen interviews.

Access to Study Participants

There were two preconditions to gaining access to study participants: (1) the approval of managers in the social worker's employing organization and (2) the social worker's informed consent. Each required information on the purpose of the study, the time commitment required of the social worker, and how confidentiality and anonymity would be protected. Contact with managers occurred initially by telephone or letter. Potential study participants were not identified. When the manager's approval for participation had been provided, I contacted potential participants.

Interview Process

Potential interviewees were initially contacted by telephone so that I could introduce the study, explain its purposes, and explore their interest in participating. Following this introduction I sent a letter of introduction to confirm the content of the telephone conversation. A second telephone contact was made to confirm interest in participation and to establish the time, date, and place of the interview. In addition, the concept of informed consent was introduced, and an informed consent form was sent to the prospective interviewee. This form was then collected, usually on the day of the interview. At the interview I reintroduced the purpose of the study, reviewed the provisions for confidentiality, and thanked the interviewee for agreeing to participate. The initial set of interviews (including pre-test interviews) occurred between June and August 1998. A second set of interviews was conducted between June and October 1999.

Reliability and Validity of the Study

This study, a scientific contribution to social work knowledge, must conform to criteria used to evaluate the soundness of any research endeavour. Characteristically, this refers to the extent to which the data collection instruments provide reliable and valid measures of the concepts under study, and the extent to which the created knowledge is transferable beyond the study sample. I audiotaped each interview and transcribed it to text in order to collect the data. I ensured the reliability of the transcript by reviewing the transcript for accuracy. Its validity as a measure of participants' thinking was confirmed by providing study participants with the opportunity to review a draft of the study's findings. Although the findings cannot be generalized beyond the study sample, they have significance for child protection practice with minority groups.

Qualitative studies require flexibility in the design process so as to respond to an evolving understanding of the phenomenon being researched. Also, the researcher's subjectivity becomes an unavoidable reality in both data collection and analysis (Flinders and Mills 1993, 186; Altheide and Johnson 1994, 496). In addition, the data and their analysis have a reciprocal influence on each other as each shapes the evolving direction of the study. This creates challenges unique to qualitative research to ensure a sound and trustworthy contribution to knowledge. All systematic inquiry into the human condition must establish the "truth value" of the research and establish its applicability, consistency, and neutrality (Marshall and Rossman 1995, 143). Qualitative research is no exception. In this respect, four questions are posed as criteria by which to judge all scientific inquiry: How credible are the particular findings of this study? How transferable and applicable are these findings to another setting or group of people? How can we be reasonably sure the findings of this study would be replicated if the study were conducted with the same participants in the same context? How can we be reasonably sure that the findings are reflective of the subjects and the inquiry itself rather than being a creation of the researcher's biases or prejudices? (Lincoln and Guba 1985).

Credibility refers to the extent to which the subject is accurately identified and described. Qualitative studies usually achieve credibility through the in-depth description of the subject. This study provides three opportunities to accurately describe the subject. These are the initial interview, the follow-up interview (where implemented), and the presentation of initial findings. In each case, inaccuracies, misunderstandings, and subtle meanings were clarified through questions and discussion with study participants.

Transferability refers to the extent to which the findings from my study can be generalized or applied to another setting or group. Since a convenience sample has been used to select study participants, the results cannot be formally generalized to child protection social workers in British Columbia or Canada. However, the absence of knowledge about child protection practice in general, in cross-cultural perspective in particular, and specifically with Aboriginal social workers and children suggests that this study has value and use in all three dimensions. It will increase understanding of cross-cultural child protection practice and will make a contribution to understanding wherever subjugated minorities are found in child welfare, including in countries such as the United States, Britain, and Australia, where black, Chicano, and Aboriginal children are overrepresented in child welfare.

Dependability refers to my attempts to account for changing research conditions as well as design changes related to the increased understanding of the subject. I provided participants with the opportunity to review the findings in order to explore changes in their responses to questions over time. That was also a means of ensuring the full comprehension of participants' views and of allowing me to establish both the level of stability and the level of change in participants' perspectives since the interview date.

Confirmability refers to whether the findings of the study could be confirmed by another. This issue is complex in qualitative work because it presumes that a second researcher could replicate exactly my observations, data collection processes, and analyses at a different point in time. It assumes that the reconstruction of identical conditions and experiences is possible. However, lived experience is changing and unstable, and its identical replication is not possible. The best alternative is clear evidence of an "analytic trail" that a second researcher could follow in order to assess the interpretations and analytic choices made by the first researcher. It also requires explicit controls to minimize bias in interpretation. These controls may include others who play "devil's advocate" and critically question my analyses, a constant check for negative instances, a purposeful search for rival hypotheses, a series of tests to check the data, and audits of data collection and analytic strategies (Marshall and Rossman 1995, 145). These strategies are further developed in the data analysis section.

In this study, my subjectivity is a fact to be acknowledged rather than ignored. Towards this end, my biases are stated in order to explicitly recognize their influence on the interpretive process. I am a social work educator and former executive director of the British Columbia

Association of Social Workers. I have a professional commitment to the practice of social work. I also have several family members who have been child protection practitioners in British Columbia (partner, brother, aunt, uncle). In addition, friends, professional colleagues, and former students of mine are engaged in child welfare practice. I have also been employed as a social development consultant to the Nuxalk Nation in Bella Coola, British Columbia, and taught Aboriginal students in an affirmative action BSW program at the University of Manitoba. These experiences create sympathy for and an interest in the challenges of child protection practice. They also create a desire to understand the difference culture can make in interpreting needs and formulating intervention. Fundamentally, I did my research with sensitivity to cultural difference and a will to recognize and record social workers' theorization and conceptualization of their practice.

Data Analysis

In a qualitative study, data analysis is a process of interpreting, conceptualizing, and making meaning out of the data. It is also a process that evolves as more information becomes available. Data analysis for *Protecting Aboriginal Children* began during the interviews, with me posing questions that were not found in the interview guide. At times, I posed a question to seek clarification or to have a participant expand upon an idea. At other times, a question tested my understanding by providing a summary of the participant's response. It also tested the accuracy of a tentative conceptualization or hypothesis by providing it, in summary form, to the participant. Data analysis continued following the interview as I recorded impressions, reflections, ideas, and questions in a notebook. A professional secretary formally transcribed the interviews, and I verified the accuracy of the transcription. The data were entered for analysis into a NUD*IST software program. An initial set of predefined coding categories was developed using the five theoretical dimensions and the questions from the interview guide. As interview content emerged that did not appear to fit these categories, additional codes were created (i.e., naturally emerging categories). Each interview was recoded a second time at an interval of two to six weeks, and the new coding was verified against the initial coding. When differences emerged, a process of careful review of the data was initiated to determine the most appropriate coding. The data were then recoded to the most appropriate code. This provided a measure of intra-rater reliability. On occasion, codes with a small amount of data were integrated into a code with a large amount of data. In general, there was not a significant reduction in the number of codes as part of the data analysis process.

The physical act of coding was also an ongoing opportunity to reflect, explore, and search for meaning in the data. I made notes by questioning, commenting, and describing emerging relationships. At the conclusion of this phase, reports were printed for each code and the data were analyzed for similarities, differences, variations, and negative instances. At this stage, data analysis was centred on the "constant comparison" of the data found within each code (Strauss and Corbin 1990). The fundamental data analysis question at this stage was, "What is going on here?" In addition, questions such as, "How might this data be interpreted, described, and conceptualized?" were also posed. I wrote a summary of the results for each code, noting similarities and differences as well as themes and silences. At the conclusion of this process, I linked codes together to correspond to the dimensions of child protection practice found in the theoretical framework. At the same time I carried on an ongoing scan of the content in order to identify possible themes, interpretations, explanations, and representations. At times, an emerging conceptualization was tested using the NUD*IST software's ability to search for a particular word or phrase. Data were summarized, interpreted, and described in relation to the representations of practice they suggested. A draft report of the findings was mailed to all participants, and all participants were contacted by telephone to invite their comments on the validity of the interpretation. Participants were invited to comment individually or in small groups at a time and location convenient to them. Revisions were made to incorporate participants' feedback and the data analysis process concluded.

Ethical Issues
Interviews with child protection practitioners demand a fundamental ethical responsibility to ensure that no harm occurs to study participants. Harm can occur through coercion to participate in the research, lack of understanding of the research purposes and procedures, a harmful research process (e.g., types of interview questions), or through the absence of anonymity and confidentiality in the reporting and publication of the research (Rubin and Babbie 1997, 60-2). My research minimized these risks in three ways:

• *Voluntary participation of participants:* From the initial telephone contact and letter of introduction to the follow-up contact and interview, participants were advised that there was no expectation, requirement, or obligation to participate. No incentives or favours for participation were extended.

- *Informed consent of participants:* The research's purposes, procedures, and time commitments were explained to prospective interviewees orally and in writing. The opportunity to ask questions and to clarify understanding of any aspect of the study was provided. A written consent form was completed before the interview.

- *Confidentiality and anonymity:* No names were used to report research findings, and any potentially identifiable references to location have been eliminated. At the request of participants, additional editing of case examples was undertaken to eliminate the potential for identification. I explained to participants the limitations to anonymity that would occur once they participated in the validation of findings focus groups. That is, their identity would be known to other study participants and quotations could be attributed to them more easily by other participants. This was explained orally and a second consent form completed before discussion of the findings began. I made every effort to limit identifying information about participants in reporting the research.

As I personally interviewed each participant, their anonymity in relation to me was not possible. The research process did not harm participants as the content of the interview involved descriptions and analyses of the professional practice of child protection. It did not ask participants to reveal sensitive information about themselves or others. With each practitioner, the employer's consent was obtained as a precondition to the initiation of the interview process. There was no risk of negative consequences to practitioners from their employer for participating in this research.

Limitations

The principal method of data collection was qualitative semi-structured interviews with nineteen child protection social workers in British Columbia. There was no direct observation of practice and no inclusion of clients' perspectives about child protection practice. *Protecting Aboriginal Children* therefore takes, as its principal source of data, the reflective analysis of practitioners. The opportunity to capture other perspectives on practice was not included. A basic selection criterion for inclusion in the study was a social work education, but there are a significant number of child protection practitioners at the Ministry of Children and Family Development and in Aboriginal organizations who do not have a social work degree. My book is therefore limited because it does not include these perspectives about practice. In addition, it does not feature extensive participation from participants in large urban centres. The study participants tended to practise in rural communities and small urban centres, although two had also practised in large urban centres. Several attempts were made, without success, to gain access to practitioners in large urban centres (Greater Vancouver and Victoria) who have extensive contact with Aboriginal children and families. In addition, it was not possible to find a male Aboriginal child protection practitioner with a social work degree. Finally, every participant did not answer all questions. At times, an interview developed a natural rhythm, and I followed the participant's thinking in the conversation rather than trying to direct it. The consequence is that not every question was asked and answered by each participant, but the major themes (as expressed by the theoretical dimensions of practice) were covered.

References

Abric, J.C. (1994). *Pratiques sociales et répresentations*. Paris: Presses Universitaires de France.

Adams, H. (1999). *Tortured people: The politics of colonization*. Rev. ed. Penticton, BC: Theytus.

Altheide, D., and J. Johnson (1994). Criteria for assessing interpretive validity in qualitative research. In N. Denzin and Y. Lincoln, eds., *Handbook of qualitative research*, 485-99. London: Sage.

Armitage, A. (1993a). Family and child welfare in First Nation communities. In B. Wharf, ed., *Rethinking child welfare in Canada*, 131-71. Toronto: McClelland and Stewart.

–. (1993b). The policy and legislative context. In B. Wharf, ed., *Rethinking child welfare in Canada*, 37-63. Toronto: McClelland and Stewart.

Armitage, A., E. Lane, F. Ricks, and B. Wharf (1988). *Evaluation of the Champagne/ Aishihik Child Welfare Pilot Project*. Victoria: University of Victoria.

Assembly of First Nations (2004). Residential School Briefing Note (for) National Chief Matthew Coon Come. Prepared by Charlene Belleau. Ottawa: The Assembly.

Barsky, A., G. Rogers, J. Krysik, and P. Langevin (1997). Evaluating the integration of social work theory and practice. *Canadian Social Work Review* 14 (2): 185-200.

Bartlett, H. (1961). *Analyzing social work practice by fields*. New York: National Association of Social Workers.

–. (1965). Social work practice. In R. Morris, ed., *Encyclopedia of social work*. 15th ed., 755-63. New York: National Association of Social Workers.

–. (1970). *The common base of social work practice*. New York: National Association of Social Workers.

Berger, P. (1977). Towards a sociological understanding of psychoanalysis. In *Facing up to modernity: Excursions in society, politics, and religion*, 23-34. New York: Basic Books.

Bertrand, L. (1993). Réflexion sur la notion de "représentation." Définir le concept pour éviter les fausses représentations. *Revue de l'Association pour la recherche qualitative* 9: 102-14.

Billig, M. (1993). Studying the thinking society: Social representations, rhetoric, and attitudes. In G.M. Breakwell and D.V. Canter, eds., *Empirical approaches to social representations*, 39-62. Oxford: Clarendon.

Boyer, P. (1992). Young and old alike: Children and the elderly are a priority in Native American cultures. *Journal of American Indian Higher Education* 3 (4): 24-6.

Breakwell, G. and D. Canter, eds. (1993). *Empirical approaches to social representations*. Oxford: Clarendon.

British Columbia (1974). *Tenth report of the Royal Commission on Family and Children's Law: Native families and the law*. Vancouver: The Commission.

British Columbia Ministry of Children and Family Development (2004). *Delegated Aboriginal Child and Family Service Agencies*. Victoria: The Ministry.

British Columbia Ministry of Human Resources (1981). *Policy and procedures manual*. Victoria: The Ministry.

Brook, P. (1997). Rush to re-organization makes another Matthew likely: The situation in child protection is as bad as it's been in decades. *Vancouver Sun*, 12 November, A21.

–. (1997). Ministry of chaos. *Vancouver Sun*, 26 November, A21.

Burford, G., and J. Hudson, eds. (2000). *Family group conferencing: New directions in community-centered child and family practice*. New York: Aldine De Gruyter.

Callahan, M. (1993). The administrative and practice context. In B. Wharf, ed., *Rethinking child welfare in Canada*, 64-97. Toronto: McClelland and Stewart.

Callahan, M., and B. Wharf (1982). *Demystifying the policy process: A case study of the development of child welfare legislation in BC*. Victoria: The authors.

Carew, R. (1979). The place of knowledge in social work activity. *British Journal of Social Work* 9 (3): 349-64.

Carniol, B. (2000). *Case critical: Challenging social services in Canada*. 4th ed. Toronto: Between the Lines.

Chrisjohn, R., S. Young, and M. Maraun (1997). *The circle game: Shadows and substance in the Indian residential school experience in Canada*. Penticton, BC: Theytus.

Community Panel, Family and Children's Services Legislation Review in British Columbia (1992). *Liberating our children, liberating our nations: Report of the Aboriginal Committee*. Victoria: BC Ministry of Social Services.

Corby, B. (1991). Sociology, social work, and child protection. In M. Davies, ed., *The sociology of social work*, 87-105. London: Routledge.

Cruickshank, D. (1985). The Berger Commission report on the protection of children: The impact on prevention of child abuse and neglect. In K. Levitt and B. Wharf, eds., *The challenge of child welfare*, 182-99. Vancouver: UBC Press.

–. (1991). The child in care. In N. Bala, J. Hornick, and R. Vogl, eds., *Canadian child welfare law: Children, families and the state*, 77-106. Toronto: Thompson Publishing.

Damm, U. (1992). Awasis Agency and adoption. In M. Tobin and C. Walmsley, eds., *Northern perspectives: Practice and education in social work*, 53-60. Winnipeg: Manitoba Association of Social Workers and the University of Manitoba Faculty of Social Work.

Department of Social Welfare (1966). *Policy and procedures manual*. Victoria, BC: Department of Social Welfare.

Deutscher, I. (1984). Choosing ancestors: Some consequences of the selection from intellectual traditions. In R. Farr and S. Moscovici, eds., *Social representations*, 71-100. Cambridge: Cambridge University Press.

Doise, W. (1986). Les représentations sociales: Définition d'un concept. In W. Doise and A. Palmonari, eds., *L'étude des représentations sociales*, 81-94. Paris: Delachaux et Niestle.

Donzelot, J. (1997). *The policing of families*. Baltimore: Johns Hopkins.

D'Souza, N. (1994). Indigenous child welfare or institutionalized colonialism? *Social Alternatives* 13 (1): 32-5.

Dumont, R. (1988). Culturally selective perceptions in child welfare decisions. *The Social Worker* 56 (4): 149-52.

Durie, H., and A. Armitage (1995). *Legislative change: The development of BC's Child, Family and Community Service Act and Child, Youth and Family Advocacy Act*. Victoria: Child, Family and Community Research Program of the School of Social Work, University of Victoria.

Duveen, G., and B. Lloyd (1993). An ethnographic approach to social representations. In G.M. Breakwell and D.V. Canter, eds., *Empirical approaches to social representations*, 90-109. Oxford: Clarendon.

Edelman, M. (1984). The political language of the helping professions. In M. Shapiro, ed., *Language and Politics*, 44-60. Oxford: Basil Blackwell.

Emler, N., and J. Ohana (1993). Studying representations in children: Just old wine in new bottles? In G.M. Breakwell and D.V. Canter, eds., *Empirical approaches to social representations*, 63-89. Oxford: Clarendon.

Epstein, L. (1994). The therapeutic idea in contemporary society. In A. Chambon and A. Irving, eds., *Essays on postmodernism and social work*, 3-18. Toronto: Canadian Scholar's Press.

Farr, R. (1993). Theory and method in the study of social representations. In G.M. Breakwell and D.V. Canter, eds., *Empirical approaches to social representations*, 15-38. Oxford: Clarendon.

Farr, R., and S. Moscovici, eds. (1984). *Social representations*. Cambridge, Paris: Cambridge University, Editions de la Maison des Sciences de l'Homme.

Flinders, D., and G. Mills, eds. (1993). *Theory and concepts in qualitative research: Perspectives from the field*. New York: Teachers College Press.

Fournier, S., and E. Crey (1997). *Stolen from our embrace: The abduction of First Nations children and the restoration of Aboriginal communities*. Vancouver: Douglas and MacIntyre.

Frankel, H. (1988). Family-centered, home-based services in child protection: A review of the research. *Social Service Review* 62 (1): 137-57.

Fraser, N., and L. Gordon (1994). A genealogy of dependency: Tracing a keyword of the US Welfare State. *Signs* 19 (21): 309-36.

Fuchs, D. (1995). Preserving and strengthening families and protecting children: Social network intervention, a balanced approach to child maltreatment. In J. Hudson and B. Galaway, eds., *Child welfare in Canada: Research and policy implications*, 113-22. Toronto: Thompson Educational.

Furniss, E. (1992). *Victims of benevolence: The dark legacy of the Williams Lake residential school*. Vancouver: Arsenal Pulp Press.

Glaser, B., and A. Strauss (1967). *The discovery of grounded theory*. Chicago: Aldine.

Gove Inquiry into Child Protection (1995). *Report of the Gove Inquiry into Child Protection*. Victoria: British Columbia Ministry of Social Services.

Groulx, L-H. (1995). Travail social et intervention en contexte d'autorité: Un renversement d'analyse. *Canadian Social Work Review* 12 (1): 98-112.

Haig-Brown, C. (1988). *Resistance and renewal: Surviving the Indian residential school.* Vancouver: Tillicum Library.

Hart, M. (1992). The Nelson House Medicine Lodge: Two cultures combined. In M. Tobin and C. Walmsley, eds., *Northern perspectives: Practice and education in social work,* 61-6. Winnipeg: Manitoba Association of Social Workers and the University of Manitoba Faculty of Social Work.

Hawthorn, H., C. Belshaw, and S. Jamieson (1958). *The Indians of British Columbia: A study of contemporary social adjustment.* Toronto: University of Toronto Press.

Herbert, E. (1995a). *An overview and analysis of First Nations child and family services in BC.* Prepared for the Gove Inquiry into Child Protection, Government of British Columbia. Vancouver: The Inquiry.

–. (1995b). *The practice of family meetings in First Nations child and family services programs.* Prepared for the Gove Inquiry into Child Protection, Government of British Columbia. Vancouver: The Inquiry.

Herzlich, C. (1981). La représentation sociale: sens du concept. In S. Moscovici, ed., *Introduction à la psychologie,* 303-25. Paris: Librairie Larousse.

Hodgson, M. (1993). Rural Yukon: Innovations in child welfare. *The Social Worker* 61 (4): 155-6.

Hudson, P. (1997). First Nations child and family services: Breaking the silence. *Canadian Ethnic Studies* 29 (1): 161-72.

Hudson, P., and B. McKenzie (1987). *Evaluation of the Dakota Ojibway Child and Family Services.* Winnipeg: Department of Northern and Indian Affairs.

Hudson, P., and S. Taylor-Henley (1987). *Agreement and disagreement: An evaluation of the Canada-Manitoba Northern Indian Child Welfare Agreement.* Winnipeg: University of Manitoba.

Hume, S. (1991). The Champagne/Aishihik Family and Children's Services: A unique community based approach to service delivery. *Northern Review* 7: 62-71.

Hutchison, E. (1987). Use of authority in direct social work practice with mandated clients. *Social Service Review* 61 (4): 581-98.

Ing, N. (1991). The effects of residential schools on native child-rearing practices. *Canadian Journal of Native Education* 18: 65-118.

Johnston, P. (1983). *Native children and the child welfare system.* Toronto: James Lorimer and the Canadian Council on Social Development.

Jones, L. (1993). Decision-making in child welfare: A critical review of the literature. *Child and Adolescent Social Work Journal* 10 (3): 241-62.

Kamerman, S. (1998). Fields of practice. In M. Mattani, C. Lowery, and C. Meyer, eds., *The foundations of social work practice.* 2nd ed., 291-311. Washington: National Association of Social Workers.

Lincoln, Y., and E. Guba (1985). *Naturalistic inquiry.* Newbury Park: Sage.

Lindsey, D. (1992). Reliability of the foster care placement decision: A review. *Research on social work practice* 2 (1): 65-80.

–. (1994). *The welfare of children.* New York: Oxford.

Lipiansky, E.M. (1991). Représentations sociales et idéologies: Analyse conceptuelle. In V. Aebischer, J-P. Deconchy, and E. Lipiansky, eds., *Idéologies et représentations sociales,* 35-63. Cousset (Fribourg), Switzerland: Editions Del Val.

Loewenberg, F., and R. Dolgoff (1992). *Ethical decisions for social work practice.* 4th ed. Itasca, IL: F.E. Peacock.

MacDonald, J. (1985). The child welfare program of the Spallumcheen Indian Band in British Columbia. In K. Levitt and B. Wharf, eds., *The challenge of child welfare*, 253-65. Vancouver: UBC Press.

–. (1993). *Community study of the Spallumcheen Band child welfare program: Interim Report.* Enderby, BC: Royal Commission on Aboriginal Peoples.

–. (1997, May). Community dimensions in child protection practice in BC. A presentation to a research seminar held at the UBC School of Social Work.

McKenzie, B. (1989). Child welfare: New models of service delivery in Canada's Native communities. *Human Services in the Rural Environment* 12 (3): 6-11.

–. (1997). Connecting policy and practice in First Nations child and family services: A Manitoba case study. In J. Pulkingham and G. Ternowetsky, eds., *Child and family policies: Struggles, strategies and options*, 100-14. Halifax: Fernwood.

McKenzie, B., and P. Hudson (1985). Native children, child welfare, and the colonization of native people. In K. Levitt and B. Wharf, eds., *The challenge of child welfare*, 125-41. Vancouver: UBC Press.

McKenzie, B., E. Seidl, and N. Bone (1995). Child and family service standards in First Nations: An action research project. *Child Welfare* 74 (3): 633-53.

Mannes, M. (1993). Seeking the balance between child protection and family preservation in Indian child welfare. *Child Welfare* 72 (2): 141-52.

Marshall, C., and G. Rossman (1995). *Designing qualitative research.* 2nd. ed. Thousand Oaks: Sage.

Maslow, A. (1968). *Towards a psychology of being.* 2nd ed. Princeton: Van Nostrand.

Mathias, J., and G. Yabsley (1991). Conspiracy of legislation: The suppression of Indian rights in Canada. In D. Jensen and C. Brooks, eds., *In celebration of our survival: The First Nations of British Columbia*, 34-47. Vancouver: UBC Press.

Miller, J. (1996). *Shingwauk's Vision.* Toronto: University of Toronto Press.

Morrissette, V., B. McKenzie, and L. Morrissette (1993). Towards an Aboriginal model of social work practice: Cultural knowledge and traditional practices. *Canadian Social Work Review* 10 (1): 91-108.

Moscovici, S. (1976). *La psychanalyse, son image, son public.* 2nd ed. Paris: Presses Universitaires de France.

–. (1984). The phenomenon of social representations. In R. Farr and S. Moscovici, eds., *Social representations,* 3-69. Cambridge, Paris: Cambridge University, Editions de la Maison des Sciences de l'Homme.

Mullaly, R. (1997). *Structural social work: Ideology, theory and practice.* 2nd. ed. Toronto: Oxford University Press.

–. (2002). *Challenging oppression: A critical social work approach.* Toronto: Oxford University Press.

National Council of Welfare (1997). *Poverty profile 1995.* Ottawa: Minister of Supply and Services Canada.

Nelson, B. (1984). *Making an issue of child abuse: Political agenda setting for social problems.* Chicago: University of Chicago.

Nelson, C., M. Kelley, D. McPherson (1985). Rediscovering support in social work practice: Lessons from Indian indigenous human service workers. *Canadian Social Work Review*: 231-48.

Office of the Child Youth and Family Advocate (1997). *Annual Report.* Victoria, BC: The Office.

–. (1997). *Annual Report.* Victoria, BC: The Office.

–. (1999). *Annual Report.* Victoria, BC: The Office.

Pallan, P. (2000). *Children's Commission: 1999 Annual Report.* Victoria, BC: The Commission.

Palmer, S. (1983). Authority: An essential part of practice. *Social Work* 2: 120-5.

Palmonari, A., and M.L. Pombeni (1984). Psychologists versus psychologists: An outlook on a professional orientation. In G.M. Stephenson and J.H. Davis, eds., *Progress in Applied Social Psychology.* Vol. 2. New York: John Wiley and Sons.

Parton, N. (1991). *Governing the family: Child care, child protection and the state.* London: Macmillan.

–. (1994). "Problematics of government," (post) modernity and social work. *British Journal of Social Work* 24: 9-32.

–, ed. (1997). *Child protection and family support: Tensions, contradictions and possibilities.* London: Routledge.

Pateman, C. (1988). The patriarchal welfare state. In A. Gutmann, ed. *Democracy and the welfare state,* 231-60. Princeton: Princeton University.

Payne, M. (1997). *Modern social work theory.* 2nd. ed. Chicago: Lyceum.

Pease, B., and J. Fook, eds. (1999). *Transforming social work practice: Postmodern critical perspectives.* London: Routledge.

Pelton, L. (1994). Is poverty a key contributor to child maltreatment? Yes! In E. Gambrill and T. Stein, eds., *Controversial issues in child welfare,* 16-28. Boston: Allyn and Bacon.

Pennell, J., and G. Burford (1997). *Family group decision making: After the conference – Progress in resolving violence and promoting well-being.* St. John's, NF: School of Social Work Memorial University.

Purvey, D. (1991). Alexandra Orphanage and Families in Crisis in Vancouver, 1892 to 1938. In R. Smamdych, G. Dodds, and A. Esau, eds., *Dimensions of childhood: Essays on the history of children and youth in Canada,* 107-33. Winnipeg: Legal Research Unit of the University of Manitoba.

Ramsay, G. (1986). Permanent planning for native Indian children in the care of the Superintendent of Family and Child Services of British Columbia. Unpublished report.

Reamer, F. (1995). *Social work values and ethics.* New York: Columbia.

Rein, M., and S.H. White (1981). Knowledge for practice. *Social Service Review* 55 (1): 1-41.

Rhodes, M. (1991). *Ethical dilemmas in social work practice.* New York: Family Service America.

Roberts, R. (1990). *Lessons from the past: Issues for social work theory.* London: Tavistock/Routledge.

Royal Commission on Aboriginal Peoples (1996). *Report of the Royal Commission on Aboriginal Peoples.* Vol. 1: *Looking Forward, Looking Back.* Ottawa: Minister of Supply and Services Canada.

–. (1996). *Report of the Royal Commission on Aboriginal Peoples.* Vol. 3: *Gathering Strength.* Ottawa: Minister of Supply and Services Canada.

Rubin, A., and E. Babbie (1997). *Research methods for social work.* Belmont, CA: Wadsworth.

Rubin, H., and I. Rubin (1995). *Qualitative interviewing: The art of hearing data.* Thousand Oaks: Sage.

Sandberry, G. (1992). The Dene Nation. In M. Tobin, and C. Walmsley, eds., *Northern perspectives: Practice and education in social work*, 25-30. Winnipeg: Faculty of Social Work University of Manitoba and the Manitoba Association of Social Workers.

Savoury, G., and K. Kufeldt (1997). Protecting children versus supporting families. *The Social Worker* 65 (3): 146-54.

Schon, D. (1993). Generative metaphor: A perspective on problem-setting in social policy. In A. Ortony, ed., *Metaphor and thought*, 137-63. 2nd ed. London: Cambridge University.

Stanbury, W. (1975). *Success and failure: Indians in urban society*. Vancouver: UBC Press.

Strauss, A., and J. Corbin (1990). *Basics of qualitative research: Grounded theory procedures and techniques*. London: Sage.

Tait, K. (1998). Job from hell: Saving abused kids. *Vancouver Province*, 2 August, 11.

Timpson, J. (1988). Depression in a native Canadian in Northwestern Ontario: Sadness, grief or spiritual illness? *Canada's Mental Health* 35 (June-September): 5-8.

Usma Nuu-Chah-Nulth Family and Child Services (1999). Usma Nuu-Chah-Nulth Family and Child Services (brochure). Port Alberni, BC: Nuu-Chah-Nulth Family and Child Services.

Vancouver Sun (1997). Social workers stay home to protest "crisis": Hundreds defy union to draw attention to shortage of front-line child protection workers, 6 March, A1.

Van Krieken, R. (1991). *Children and the state: Social control and the formation of Australian child welfare*. North Sydney: Allen and Unwin.

Verquerre, R. (1989). Représentations de l'enfant, attitudes éducatives, comportements éducatifs. PhD diss., Sciences Humaines, Sorbonne, Paris.

Wagner, W., F. Elejabarrieta, and I. Lahnsteiner (1995). How sperm dominates the ovum–objectification by metaphor in the social representation of conception. *European Journal of Social Psychology* 25: 671-88.

Walmsley, C. (1987). Changing the future: A social development plan for the Nuxalk Nation. Vancouver: unpublished report.

Wares, D., and A. Dobrec (1992). Job satisfaction, practice skills, and supervisory skills of administrators of Indian child welfare programs. *Child Welfare* 71 (5): 405-19.

Wares, D., K. Wedel, J. Rosenthal, and A. Dobrec (1994). Indian child welfare: A multicultural challenge. *Journal of Multicultural Social Work* 3 (3): 1-15.

Weisman, M. (1994). When parents are not in the best interests of the child. *Atlantic Monthly* 274 (1): 42-63.

Wharf, B. (1991). Community, culture, and control: Themes for the social services in northern communities. *Northern Review* 7: 132-42.

–. (1995). Organizing and delivering child welfare services: The contributions of research. In J. Hudson and B. Galaway, eds., *Child welfare in Canada: Research and policy implications*, 2-12. Toronto: Thompson Educational Publishing.

–., ed. (2002). *Community work approaches to child welfare*. Toronto: Broadview.

York, G. (1990). *The dispossessed: Life and death in Native Canada*. Toronto: Little, Brown and Company.

Zani, B. (1987). The psychiatric nurse: A social psychological study of a profession facing institutional changes. *Social Behaviour* 2: 87-98.

–. (1993). Social representations of mental illness: Lay and professional perspectives. In G.M. Breakwell and D.V. Canter, eds., *Empirical approaches to social representations*, 315-30. Oxford: Clarendon.

Zylberberg, P. (1991). Who should make child protection decisions for the native community? *Windsor Yearbook of Access to Justice* 11: 74-103.

Index

Printed and bound in Canada by Friesens

Set in Stone by Artegraphica Design Co. Ltd.

Copy editor: Joanne Richardson

Proofreader: Dianne Tiefensee

Indexer: Adrian Mather